Charles Kingsley

Three lectures delivered at the Royal institution

On the ancien regime as it existed on the continent before the French revolution

Charles Kingsley

Three lectures delivered at the Royal institution
On the ancien regime as it existed on the continent before the French revolution

ISBN/EAN: 9783742807755

Manufactured in Europe, USA, Canada, Australia, Japa

Cover: Foto ©ninafisch / pixelio.de

Manufactured and distributed by brebook publishing software
(www.brebook.com)

Charles Kingsley

Three lectures delivered at the Royal institution

THREE LECTURES

DELIVERED AT THE ROYAL INSTITUTION,

ON THE

ANCIEN REGIME

AS IT EXISTED ON THE CONTINENT BEFORE THE
FRENCH REVOLUTION.

BY

C. KINGSLEY, M.A.

PROFESSOR OF MODERN HISTORY IN THE UNIVERSITY OF CAMBRIDGE.

London:

MACMILLAN AND CO.

1867.

PREFACE.

THE Rules of the Royal Institution forbid (and wisely) religious or political controversy. It was therefore impossible for me, in these Lectures, to say much which had to be said, in drawing a just and complete picture of the Ancien Regime in France. The passages inserted between brackets, which bear on religious matters, were accordingly not spoken at the Royal Institution.

But more. It was impossible for me, in these Lectures, to bring forward as fully as I could have wished, the contrast between the Continental nations and England, whether now, or during the eighteenth century. But that contrast cannot be too carefully studied at the present moment. In proportion as it is seen and understood, will the fear of revolution (if such exists) die out among the wealthier

classes ; and the wish for it (if such exists) among
the poorer; and a large extension of the suffrage
will be looked on as—what it actually is—a safe
and harmless concession to the wishes—and, as I
hold, to the just rights—of a large portion of the
British nation.

There exists in Britain now, as far as I can see,
no one of those evils which brought about the
French Revolution. There is no wide-spread
misery, and therefore no wide-spread discontent,
among the classes who live by hand-labour. The
legislation of the last generation has been steadily
in favour of the poor, as against the rich; and it
is even more true now than it was in 1789, that
—as Arthur Young told the French mob which
stopped his carriage—the rich pay many taxes
(over and above the poor-rates, a direct tax on the
capitalist in favour of the labourer) more than are
paid by the poor. "In England" (says M. De
Tocqueville of even the eighteenth century) "the
poor man enjoyed the privilege of exemption from
taxation : in France, the rich." Equality before the
law is as well-nigh complete as it can be, where

some are rich and others poor; and the only privileged class, it sometimes seems to me, is the pauper, who has neither the responsibility of self-government, nor the toil of self-support.

A minority of malcontents, some justly, some unjustly angry with the present state of things, will always exist in this world. But a majority of malcontents we shall never have, as long as the workmen are allowed to keep untouched and unthreatened their rights of free speech, free public meeting, free combination for all purposes which do not provoke a breach of the peace. There may be (and probably are) to be found in London and the large towns, some of those revolutionary propagandists who have terrified and tormented Continental statesmen since the year 1815. But they are far fewer in number than in 1848; far fewer still (I believe) than in 1831; and their habits, notions, temper, whole mental organization, is so utterly alien to that of the average Englishman, that it is only the sense of wrong which can make him take counsel with them, or make common cause with them. Meanwhile, every man who is

admitted to a vote, is one more person withdrawn
from the temptation to disloyalty, and enlisted in
maintaining the powers that be—when they are
in the wrong, as well as when they are in the
right. For every Englishman is by his nature
conservative; slow to form an opinion; cautious
in putting it into effect; patient under evils which
seem irremediable; persevering in abolishing such
as seem remediable; and then only too ready
to acquiesce in the earliest practical result; to
"rest and be thankful." His faults, as well as
his virtues, make him anti-revolutionary. He is
generally too dull to take in a great idea; and if
he does take it in, often too selfish to apply it to
any interest save his own. But now and then,
when the sense of actual injury forces upon him a
great idea, like that of Free-trade, or of Parlia-
mentary Reform, he is indomitable, however slow
and patient, in translating his thought into fact;
and they will not be wise statesmen who resist
his dogged determination. If at this moment he
demands an extension of the suffrage eagerly and
even violently, the wise statesman will give at

once, gracefully and generously, what the Englishman will certainly obtain one day, if he has set
his mind upon it. If, on the other hand, he asks
for it calmly, then the wise statesman (instead of
mistaking English reticence for apathy) will listen
to his wishes all the more readily; seeing in the
moderation of the demand, the best possible
guarantee for moderation in the use of the thing
demanded.

And, be it always remembered, that in introducing these men into "the balance of the Con-
stitution," we introduce no unknown quantity.
Statesmen ought to know them, if they know
themselves; to judge what the working man would
do, by what they do themselves. He who imputes
virtues to his own class, imputes them also to the
labouring class. He who imputes vices to the
labouring class, imputes them to his own class.
For both are not only of the same flesh and blood,
but, what is infinitely more important, of the same
spirit; of the same race; in innumerable cases, of
the same ancestors. For centuries past, the most
able of these men have been working upwards

into the middle class, and through it, often, to the
highest dignities, and the highest family connexions;
and the whole nation knows how they have com-
ported themselves therein. And, by a reverse
process (of which the physiognomist and gene-
alogist can give abundant proof), the weaker
members of that class which was dominant during
the Middle Age have been sinking downward,
often to the rank of mere day-labourers, and
carrying downward with them—sometimes in a
very tragical and pathetic fashion—somewhat of
the dignity and the refinement which they had
learnt from their ancestors.

Thus has the English nation (and as far as I can
see the Scotch likewise) become more homogeneous
than any nation of the Continent, if we except
France since the extermination of the Frankish
nobility. And for that very reason, as it seems
to me, it is more fitted than any other European
nation for the exercise of equal political rights;
and not to be debarred of them by arguments
drawn from countries which have been governed—
as England has not been—by a caste.

The civilization, not of mere book-learning, but of the heart; all that was once meant by "manners"—good breeding, high feeling, respect for self and respect for others—are just as common (as far as I have seen) among the hand-workers of England and Scotland, as among any other class; the only difference is, that these qualities develop more early in the richer classes, owing to that severe discipline of our public schools, which makes mere lads often fit to govern, because they have learnt to obey: while they develop later—generally not till middle age—in the classes who have not gone through in their youth that Spartan training, and who, indeed (from a mistaken conception of liberty), would not endure it for a day. This and other social drawbacks which are but too patent, retard the manhood of the working classes. That it should be so, is a wrong. For if a citizen have one right above all others to demand anything of his country, it is, that he should be educated; that whatever capabilities he may have in him, however small, should have their fair and full chance of development. But the cause of the wrong is not the existence of a caste, or a privileged class, or of anything save the plain fact, that some men will be always able to pay more for their children's education than others; and that those children will, inevitably, win in the struggle of life.

Meanwhile, in this fact is to be found the most weighty, if not the only argument against manhood suffrage, which would admit many—but too many, alas!—who are still mere boys in mind. To a reasonable household suffrage it cannot apply. The man who (being almost certainly married, and having children) can afford to rent a £5 tenement in a town, or in the country either, has seen quite enough of life, and learnt quite enough from it, to form a very fair judgment of the man who offers to represent him in Parliament; because he has learnt, not merely something of his own interest, or that of his class, but—what is infinitely more important —the difference between the pretender and the honest man.

The causes of this state of society, which is peculiar to Britain, must be sought far back in the

ages. It would seem that the distinction between
"earl and churl" (the noble and the non-noble
freeman) was crushed out in this island by the two
Norman conquests—that of the Anglo-Saxon nobility by Sweyn and Canute; and that of the
Anglo-Danish nobility by William and his Frenchmen. Those two terrible calamities following each
other in the short space of fifty years, seem to have
welded together, by a community of suffering, all
ranks and races, at least south of the Tweed; and
when the English rose after the storm, they rose
as one homogeneous people, never to be governed
again by an originally alien race. The English
nobility were, from the time of Magna_Charta,
rather an official nobility, than, as in most continental countries, a separate caste; and whatever
caste tendencies had developed themselves before
the Wars of the Roses (as such are certain to do
during centuries of continued wealth and power),
were crushed out by the great revolutionary events
of the next hundred years. Especially did the
discovery of the New World, the maritime struggle
with Spain, the outburst of commerce and colo-

nization during the reigns of Elizabeth and James,
help toward this good result. It was in vain for
the Lord Oxford of the day, sneering at Raleigh's
sudden elevation, to complain that as on the vir-
ginals, so in the State, " Jacks went up, and heads
went down." The proudest noblemen were not
ashamed to have their ventures on the high seas,
and to send their younger sons trading, or buc-
caneering, under the conduct of low-born men like
Drake, who " would like to see the gentleman
that would not set his hand to a rope, and hale
and draw with the mariners." Thus sprang up
that respect for, even fondness for, severe bodily
labour, which the educated class of no nation save
our own has ever felt; and which has stood them
in such good stead, whether at home or abroad.
Thus, too, sprang up the system of society by
which (as the ballad sets forth) the squire's son
might be a " 'prentice good," and marry

> " The bailiff's daughter dear
> That dwelt at Islington,"

without tarnishing, as he would have done on the

Continent, the scutcheon of his ancestors. That
which has saved England from a central despotism,
such as crushed, during the eighteenth century,
every nation on the Continent, is the very
same peculiarity which makes the advent of the
masses to a share in political power safe and
harmless; namely, the absence of caste, or rather
(for there is sure to be a moral fact underlying
and causing every political fact) the absence
of that wicked pride which perpetuates caste;
forbidding those to intermarry, whom nature and
fact pronounce to be fit mates before God and
man.

These views are not mine only. They have
been already set forth so much more forcibly by
M. De Tocqueville, that I should have thought it
unnecessary to talk about them, were not the
rhetorical phrases, "Caste," "Privileged Classes,"
"Aristocratic Exclusiveness," and suchlike, bandied
about again just now, as if they represented facts.
If there remain in this kingdom any facts which
correspond to those words, let them be abolished
as speedily as possible: but that such do remain

was not the opinion of the master of modern political philosophy, M. De Tocqueville.

He expresses his surprise " that the fact which distinguishes England from all other modern nations, and which alone can throw light on her peculiarities, . . . has not attracted more attention, . . . and that habit has rendered it, as it were, imperceptible to the English themselves—that England was the only country in which the system of caste had been not only modified, but effectually destroyed. The nobility and the middle classes followed the same business, embraced the same professions, and, what is far more significant, intermarried with each other. The daughter of the greatest nobleman" (and this, if true of the eighteenth century, has become far more true of the nineteenth) "could already, without disgrace, marry a man of yesterday." . . .

" It has often been remarked that the English nobility has been more prudent, more able, and less exclusive than any other. It would have been much nearer the truth to say, that in England, for a very long time past, no nobility, properly so

called, have existed, if we take the word in the
ancient and limited sense it has everywhere else
retained." . . .

"For several centuries the word gentleman"
(he might have added, burgess) "has altogether
changed its meaning in England; and the word
roturier has ceased to exist. In each succeeding
century it is applied to persons placed somewhat
lower in the social scale" (as the "bagman" of
Pickwick has become, and has deserved to become,
the "commercial gentleman" of our day). "At
length it travelled with the English to America,
where it is used to designate every citizen indis-
criminately. Its history is that of democracy
itself." . . .

"If the middle classes of England, instead of
making war upon the aristocracy, have remained
so intimately connected with it, it is not specially
because the aristocracy is open to all, but rather,
because its outline was indistinct, and its limit
unknown: not so much because any man might
be admitted into it, as because it was impossible
to say with certainty when he took rank there:

b

so that all who approached it might look on themselves as belonging to it ; might take part in its rule, and derive either lustre or profit from its influence."

Just so; and therefore the middle classes of Britain, of whatever their special political party, are conservative in the best sense of that word.

For there are not three, but only two, classes in England; namely, rich and poor :—those who live by capital (from the wealthiest landlord to the smallest village shopkeeper); and those who live by hand-labour. Whether the division between those two classes is increasing or not, is a very serious question. Continued legislation in favour of the hand-labourer, and a beneficence toward him, when in need, such as no other nation on earth has ever shown, have done much to abolish the moral division. But the social division has surely been increased during the last half century, by the inevitable tendency, both in commerce and agriculture, to employ one large capital, where several small ones would have been employed a century ago. The large manufactory, the large shop, the large estate, the large farm, swallows up the small ones. The yeoman, the thrifty squatter who could work at two or three trades as well as till his patch of moor, the hand-loom weaver, the skilled village craftsman, have all but disappeared. The handworker, finding it more and more difficult to invest his savings, has been more and more tempted to squander them. To rise to the dignity of a capitalist, however small, was growing impossible to him, till the rise of that co-operative movement, which will do more than any social or political impulse in our day for the safety of English society, and the loyalty of the English working classes. And meanwhile—ere that movement shall have spread throughout the length and breadth of the land, and have been applied, as it surely will be some day, not only to distribution, not only to manufacture, but to agriculture likewise—till then, the best judges of the working men's worth must be their employers; and especially the employers of the northern manufacturing population. What their judgment is, is sufficiently notorious. Those who depend most on the working men, who have

the best opportunities of knowing them, trust them
most thoroughly. As long as great manufacturers
stand forward as the political sponsors of their own
workmen, it behoves those who cannot have had
their experience, to consider their opinion as con-
clusive. As for that "influence of the higher
classes" which is said to be endangered just now;
it will exist, just as much as it deserves to exist.
Any man who is superior to the many, whether in
talents, education, refinement, wealth, or anything
else, will always be able to influence a number of
men—and if he thinks it worth his while, of votes
—by just and lawful means. And as for unjust and
unlawful means, let those who prefer them keep up
heart. The world will go on much as it did before;
and be always quite bad enough to allow bribery
and corruption, jobbery and nepotism, quackery
and arrogance, their full influence over our home
and foreign policy. An extension of the suffrage,
however wide, will not bring about the millennium.
It will merely make a large number of Englishmen
contented and loyal, instead of discontented and
disloyal. It may make, too, the educated and

wealthy classes wiser, by awakening a wholesome
fear—perhaps, it may be, by awakening a chivalrous emulation. It may put the younger men of
the present aristocracy upon their mettle, and stir
them up to prove that they are not in the same
effete condition as was the French noblesse in 1789.
It may lead them to take the warnings which have
been addressed to them, for the last thirty years,
by their truest friends—often by kinsmen of their
own. It may lead them to ask themselves why, in
a world which is governed by a just God, such
great power as is palpably theirs at present is entrusted to them, save that they may do more work,
and not less, than other men, under the penalties
pronounced against those to whom much is given,
and of whom much is required. It may lead
them to discover that they are in a world where
it is not safe to sit under the tree, and let the ripe
fruit drop into your mouth ; where the "competition of species" works with ruthless energy among
all ranks of being, from kings upon their thrones,
to the weeds upon the waste ; where "he that is
not hammer, is sure to be anvil ;" and he who will

not work, neither shall he eat.   It may lead them
to devote that energy (in which they surpass
so far the continental aristocracies) to something
better than out-door amusements or in-door dilet-
tantisms. There are those among them who, like
one section of the old French noblesse, content
themselves with mere complaints of " the revolutionary tendencies of the age." Let them beware
in time; for when the many are on the march,
the few who stand still are certain to be walked
over. There are those among them who, like
another section of the French noblesse, are ready,
more generously than wisely, to throw away their
own social and political advantages, and play (for
it will never be really more than playing) at democracy. Let them, too, beware. The penknife
and the axe should respect each other; for they
were wrought from the same steel: but the penknife will not be wise in trying to fell trees. Let
them accept their own position, not in conceit and
arrogance, but in fear and trembling; and see if
they cannot play the man therein, and save their
own class ; and with it, much which it has needed

many centuries to accumulate and to organize, and without which no nation has yet existed for a single century. They are no more like the old French noblesse, than are the commercial class like the old French bourgeoisie, or the labouring like the old French peasantry. Let them prove that fact by their deeds during the next generation; or sink into the condition of mere rich men, exciting, by their luxury and laziness, nothing but envy and contempt.

Meanwhile, behind all classes and social forces—I had almost said, above them all—stands a fourth estate, which will, ultimately, decide the form which English society is to take: a Press as different from the literary class of the Ancien Regime, as is everything else English; and different in this —that it is free.

The French Revolution, like every revolution (it seems to me) which has convulsed the nations of Europe for the last eighty years, was caused immediately—whatever may have been its more remote causes—by the suppression of thought; or, at least, by a sense of wrong among those who

thought. A country where every man, be he fool
or wise, is free to speak that which is in him, can
never suffer a revolution. The folly blows itself
off like steam, in harmless noise; the wisdom
becomes part of the general intellectual stock of
the nation, and prepares men for gradual, and
therefore for harmless, change.

As long as the press is free, a nation is guaranteed
against sudden and capricious folly, either from
above, or from below. As long as the press is free,
a nation is guaranteed against the worse evil of
persistent and obstinate folly, cloaking itself under
the venerable shapes of tradition and authority.
For under a free press, a nation must ultimately
be guided not by a caste, not by a class, not by
mere wealth, not by the passions of a mob: but
by mind; by the net result of all the common-
sense of its members; and in the present default
of genius, which is un-common sense, common-
sense seems to be the only, if not the best, safe-
guard for poor humanity.

THREE LECTURES

ON

THE ANCIEN REGIME

Delivered at the ROYAL INSTITUTION, *in January,* 1867.

LECTURE I.

CASTE.

THESE Lectures are meant to be comments on the state of France before the French Revolution. To English society, past or present, I do not refer. For reasons, which I have set forth at length in an introductory discourse, there never was any Ancien Regime in England.

Therefore, when the Stuarts tried to establish in England a system which might have led to a political condition like that of the Continent, all classes combined and exterminated them; while the course of English society went on as before.

B

On the contrary, England was the mother of every movement which undermined, and at last destroyed, the Ancien Regime.

From England went forth those political theories which, transmitted from America to France, became the principles of the French Revolution. From England went forth the philosophy of Locke, with all its immense results. It is noteworthy, that when Voltaire tries to persuade people, in a certain famous passage, that philosophers do not care to trouble the world—of the ten names to whom he does honour, seven names are English. " It is," he says, " neither Montaigne, nor Locke, nor Boyle, nor Spinoza, nor Hobbes, nor Lord Shaftesbury, nor Mr. Collins, nor Mr. Toland, nor Fludd, nor Baker, who have carried the torch of discord into their countries." It is worth notice, that not only are the majority of these names English: but that they belong not to the latter, but to the former half of the eighteenth century; and indeed, to the latter half of the seventeenth.

So it was with that Inductive Physical Science, which helped more than all to break up the superstitions of the Ancien Regime, and to set man face to face with the facts of the universe. From England, toward the end of the seventeenth century, it was promulgated by such men as Newton, Boyle, Sydenham, Ray, and the first founders of our Royal Society.

In England, too, arose the great religious movements of the seventeenth and eighteenth centuries—and especially that of a body which I can never mention without most deep respect—the Society of Friends. At a time when the greater part of the Continent was sunk in spiritual sleep, these men were reasserting doctrines concerning man, and his relation to his Creator, which, whether or not all believe them (as I believe them) to be founded on eternal fact, all must confess to have been of incalculable benefit to the cause of humanity and civilization.

From England, finally, about the middle of the eighteenth century, went forth—promulgated by English noblemen—that freemasonry which seems to have been the true parent of all the secret societies of Europe. Of this curious question, more hereafter. But enough has been said to show that England, instead of falling, at any period, into the stagnation of the Ancien Regime, was, from the middle of the seventeenth century, in a state of intellectual growth and ferment which communicated itself finally to the Continental nations. This is the special honour of England; universally confessed at the time. It was to England that the slowly awakening nations looked, as the source of all which was noble, true, and free, in the dawning future.

It will be seen, from what I have said, that I consider the Ancien Regime to begin in the seventeenth century. I should date its commencement —as far as that of anything so vague, unsystematic, indeed anarchic, can be defined—from the end of the Thirty Years' War, and the peace of Westphalia in 1648.

For by that time, the mighty spiritual struggles and fierce religious animosities of the preceding century had worn themselves out. And, as always happens, to a period of earnest excitement had succeeded one of weariness, disgust, half-unbelief in the many questions for which so much blood had been shed. No man had come out of the battle with altogether clean hands: some, not without changing sides more than once. The war had ended as one, not of nations, not even of zealots, but of mercenaries. The body of Europe had been pulled in pieces between them all; and the poor soul thereof — as was to be expected — had fled out through the gaping wounds. Life, mere existence, was the most pressing need. If men could — in the old prophet's words — find the life of their hand, they were content. High and low only asked to be let live. The poor asked it — slaughtered on a hundred battle-fields, burnt out of house and home: vast tracts of the centre of Europe were lying desert; the population was diminished for several generations. The trading classes, ruined by the long war, only asked to be let live, and make a little money. The nobility, too, only asked to be let live. They had lost, in the long struggle, not only often lands and power, but their ablest and bravest men; and a weaker and meaner generation was left behind, to do the governing of the

world. Let them live, and keep what they had.
If signs of vigour still appeared in France, in the
wars of Louis **XIV**. they were feverish, factitious,
temporary — soon, as the event proved, to droop
into the general exhaustion. If wars were still to
be waged, they were to be wars of succession,
wars of diplomacy ; not wars of principle, waged
for the mightiest invisible interests of man. The
exhaustion was general ; and to it we must attribute
alike the changes and the conservatism of the
Ancien Regime. To it is owing that growth of a
centralizing despotism, and of arbitrary regal
power, which M. De Tocqueville has set forth in
a book which I shall have occasion often to quote.
To it is owing, too, that longing, which seems
to us childish, after ancient forms, etiquettes,
dignities, court costumes, formalities diplomatic,
legal, ecclesiastical. Men clung to them as to
keepsakes of the past—revered relics of more in-
telligible and better ordered times. If the spirit
had been beaten out of them in a century of battle, that was all the more reason for keeping up
the letter. They had had a meaning once, a life

once : perhaps there was a little life left in them still; perhaps the dry bones would clothe themselves with flesh once more, and stand upon their feet. At least it was useful that the common people should so believe. There was good hope that the simple masses, seeing the old dignities and formalities still parading the streets, should suppose that they still contained men, and were not mere wooden figures, dressed artistically in official costume. And, on the whole, that hope was not deceived. More than a century of bitter experience was needed ere the masses discovered that their ancient rulers were like the suits of armour in the Tower of London — empty iron astride of wooden steeds, and armed with lances which every ploughboy could wrest out of their hands, and use in his own behalf.

The mistake of the masses was pardonable. For those suits of armour had once held living men ; strong, brave, wise ; men of an admirable temper ; doing their work according to their light, not altogether well—what man does that on earth ?—but well enough to make themselves necessary to, and loyally followed by, the masses whom they ruled. No one can read fairly the 'Gesta Dei per Francos in Oriente,' or the deeds of the French Nobility in their wars with England, or those tales—however legendary—of the mediæval knights, which form so noble an element in German literature, without seeing, that however black were these men's occasional crimes, they were a truly noble race, the old Nobility of the continent ; a race which ruled simply because without them, there would have been nought but anarchy and barbarism. To their chivalrous ideal they were too often, perhaps for the most part, untrue : but, partial and defective as it is, it is an ideal such as never entered into the mind of Celt or Gaul, Hun or Sclav ; one which seems continuous with the spread of the Teutonic conquerors. They ruled because they did practically raise the ideal of humanity in the countries which they conquered, a whole stage higher. They ceased to rule when they were, through their own sins, caught up and surpassed in the race of progress by the classes below them.

But, even when at its best, their system of

government had in it—like all human invention—
original sin ; an unnatural and unrighteous element,
which was certain, sooner or later, to produce decay and ruin. The old Nobility of Europe was not
a mere aristocracy. It was a caste : a race not
intermarrying with the races below it. It was not
a mere aristocracy. For that, for the supremacy
of the best men, all societies strive, or profess to
strive. And such a true aristocracy may exist
independent of caste, or the hereditary principle
at all. We may conceive an Utopia, governed by
an aristocracy which should be really democratic ;
which should use, under developed forms, that
method which made the mediæval priesthood the
one great democratic institution of old Chris-
tendom; bringing to the surface and utilizing
the talents and virtues of all classes, even to
the lowest. We may conceive an aristocracy
choosing out, and gladly receiving into its own
ranks as equals, every youth, every maiden, who
was distinguished by intellect, virtue, valour, beauty,
without respect to rank or birth ; and rejecting
in turn, from its own ranks, each of its own

children who fell below some lofty standard, and
showed by weakliness, dulness, or baseness, in-
capacity for the post of guiding and elevating
their fellow-citizens. Thus would arise a true
aristocracy; a governing body of the really most
worthy—the most highly organised in body and
in mind—perpetually recruited from below: from
which, or from any other ideal, we are yet a few
thousand years distant.

But the old Ancien Regime would have shud-
dered, did shudder, at such a notion. The supreme
class was to keep itself pure, and avoid all taint of
darker blood, shutting its eyes to the fact that
some of its most famous heroes had been born
of such left-handed marriages as that of Robert
of Normandy with the tanner's daughter of
Falaise. " Some are so curious in this behalf,"
says quaint old Burton, writing about 1650, " as
these old Romans, our modern Venetians, Dutch,
and French, that if two parties dearly love, the one
noble, the other ignoble, they may not, by their
laws, match, though equal otherwise in years, for-
tunes, education, and all good affection. In Ger-

many, except they can prove their gentility by
three descents, they scorn to match with them.
A nobleman must marry a noblewoman ; a baron,
a baron's daughter ; a knight, a knight's. As sla-
ters sort their slates, do they degrees and families."
And doubtless this theory—like all which have
held their ground for many centuries—at first represented a fact. These castes were, at first,
actually superior to the peoples over whom they
ruled. I cannot, as long as my eyes are open,
yield to the modern theory of the equality—indeed
of the non-existence—of races. Holding, as I do, the
primeval unity of the human race, I see in that race
the same inclination to sport into fresh varieties, the
same competition of species between those varieties,
which Mr. Darwin has pointed out among plants
and mere animals. A distinguished man arises ;
from him a distinguished family ; from it a distinguished tribe, stronger, cunninger than those around.
It asserts its supremacy over its neighbours at first
exactly as a plant or animal would do, by destroying, and, where possible, eating them ; next, having
grown more prudent, by enslaving them ; next,

having gained a little morality in addition to its
prudence, by civilising them, raising them more or
less toward its own standard. And thus, in every
land, civilization and national life has arisen out of
the patriarchal state ; and the Eastern scheik, with
his wives, free and slave, and his hundreds of
fighting men born in his house, is the type of all
primæval rulers. He is the best man of his horde—
in every sense of the word best; and whether he
have a right to rule them or not, they consider that
he has, and are the better men for his guidance.

Whether this ought to have been the history of
primæval civilization, is a question not to be determined here. That it is the history thereof, is surely
patent to any one who will imagine to himself
what must have been. In the first place, the
strongest and cunningest savage must have had
the chance of producing children more strong and
cunning than the average: he would have—the
strongest savage has still—the power of obtaining
a wife, or wives, superior in beauty and in household skill, which involves superiority of intellect ;
and therefore his children would—some of them at

least—be superior to the average, both from the father's and the mother's capacities. They again would marry select wives ; and their children again would do the same ; till, in a very few generations, a family would have established itself, considerably superior to the rest of the tribe in body and mind, and become assuredly its ruling race.

Again, if one of that race invented a new weapon, a new mode of tillage, or aught else which gave him power, that would add to the superiority of his whole family. For the invention would be jealously kept among them as a mystery, a hereditary secret. To this simple cause, surely, is to be referred the system of hereditary caste occupations, whether in Egypt or in Hindoostan. To this, too, the fact that alike in Greek and in Teutonic legend the chief so often appears, not merely as the best warrior and best minstrel, but as the best smith, armourer, and handicraftsman of his tribe. If, however, the inventor happened to be a low-born genius, its advantages would still accrue to the ruling race. For nothing could be more natural or more easy— as more than one legend intimates—than that the king should extort the new secret from his subject, and then put him to death to prevent any further publicity.

Two great inventive geniuses we may see dimly through the abysses of the past, both of whom must have become in their time great chiefs, founders of mighty aristocracies—it may be, worshipped after their death as gods.

The first, who seems to have existed after the age in which the black race colonized Australia, must have been surely a man worthy to hold rank with our Brindleys, Watts, and Stephensons. For he invented (and mind, one man must have invented the thing first, and by the very nature of it, invented it all at once) an instrument so singular, unexpected, unlike anything to be seen in nature, that I wonder it has not been called, like the plough, the olive, or the vine, a gift of the immortal gods: and yet an instrument so simple, so easy, and so perfect, that it spread over all races in Europe and America, and no substitute could be found for it till the latter part of the fifteenth century. Yes, a great genius was he, and the consequent founder of a great aristocracy and a conquering race, who first invented for himself and his children after him a—bow and arrow.

The next—whether before or after the first in time, it suits me to speak of him in second place —was the man who was the potential ancestor of the whole Ritterschaft, Chivalry, and knightly caste of Europe; the man who first, finding a foal upon the steppe, deserted by its dam, brought it home, and reared it; and then bethought him of the happy notion of making it draw—presumably by its tail —a fashion which endured long in Ireland, and had to be forbidden by law, I think as late as the sixteenth century. A great aristocrat must that man have become. A greater still he who first substituted the bit for the halter. A greater still he who first thought of wheels. A greater still he who conceived the yoke and pole for bearing up his chariot; for that same yoke, and pole, and chariot, became the peculiar instrument of conquerors like him who mightily oppressed the children of Israel, for he had nine hundred chariots of iron. Egyptians, Syrians, Assyrians, Greeks, Romans—

none of them improved on the form of the conquering biga, till it was given up by a race who preferred a pair of shafts to their carts, and who had learnt to ride instead of drive. A great aristocrat, again, must he have been among those latter races who first conceived the notion of getting on his horse's back, accommodating his motions to the beast's, and becoming a centaur, half-man, half-horse. That invention must have tended, in the first instance, as surely toward democracy as did the invention of firearms. A tribe of riders must have been always, more or less, equal and free. Equal, because a man on a horse would feel himself a man indeed ; because the art of riding called out an independence, a self-help, a skill, a consciousness of power, a personal pride and vanity, which would defy slavery. Free, because a tribe of riders might be defeated, exterminated, but never enchained. They could never become glebæ adscripti, bound to the soil, as long as they could take horse and saddle, and away. History gives us more than one glimpse of such tribes—the scourge and terror of the non-riding races with whom they came in contact.

Some, doubtless, remember how in the wars between Alfred and the Danes, "the army" (the Scandinavian invaders) again and again horse themselves, steal away by night from the Saxon infantry, and ride over the land (whether in England or in France), "doing unspeakable evil." To that special instinct of horsemanship, which still distinguishes their descendants, we may attribute mainly the Scandinavian settlement of the north and east of England. Some, too, may recollect the sketch of the primæval Hun, as he first appeared to the astonished and disgusted old Roman soldier Ammianus Marcellinus; the visages "more like cakes than faces;" the "figures like those which are hewn out with an axe on the poles at bridge-ends;" the rat-skin coats, which they wore till they rot off their limbs; their steaks of meat cooked between the saddle and the thigh; the little horses on which " they eat and drink, buy and sell, and sleep lying forward along his narrow neck, and indulging in every variety of dream." And over and above, and more important politically, the common councils " held on horseback, under the authority of no king,

c

but content with the irregular government of nobles, under whose leading they force their way through all obstacles." A race—like those Cossacks who are probably their lineal descendants—to be feared, to be hired, to be petted, but not to be conquered.

Instances nearer home of free equestrian races we have in our own English borderers, among whom (as Mr. Froude says) the farmers and their farm-servants had but to snatch their arms and spring into their saddles, and they became at once the Northern Horse, famed as the finest light cavalry in the world. And equal to them—superior even, if we recollect that they preserved their country's freedom for centuries against the superior force of England—were those troops of Scots who, century after century, swept across the border on their little garrons, their bag of oatmeal hanging by the saddle, with the iron griddle whereon to bake it; careless of weather and of danger: men too swift to be exterminated, too independent to be enslaved.

But if horsemanship had, in these cases, a levelling tendency, it would have the very opposite when a riding tribe conquered a non-riding one. The conquerors would, as much as possible, keep the art and mystery of horsemanship hereditary among themselves, and become a Ritterschaft or chivalrous caste. And they would be able to do so: because the conquered race would not care or dare to learn the new and dangerous art. There are persons, even in England, who can never learn to ride. There are whole populations in Europe, even now, when races have become almost indistinguishably mixed, who seem unable to learn. And this must have been still more the case, when the races were more strongly separated in blood and habits. So the Teutonic chief, with his gesitha, comites, or select band of knights, who had received from him, as Tacitus has it, the war-horse and the lance, established himself as the natural ruler—and oppressor—of the non-riding populations; first over the aborigines of Germany proper, tribes who seem to have been enslaved, and their names lost, before the time of Tacitus; and then over the non-riding Romans and Gauls to the South and West, and the Wendish and

Sclavonic tribes to the East. Very few in numbers,
but mighty in their unequalled capacity of body
and mind, and in their terrible horsemanship, the
Teutonic Ritterschaft literally rode roughshod over
the old world; never checked, but when they came
in contact with the free riding hordes of the Eastern
steppes; and so established an equestrian caste, of
which the ἱππεῖς of Athens and the Equites of
Rome had been only hints ending in failure and
absorption.

Of that equestrian caste the symbol was the
horse. The favourite, and therefore the chosen
sacrifice of Odin, their ancestor and God, the
horse's flesh was eaten at the sacrificial meal;
the horse's head, hung on the ash in Odin's wood,
gave forth oracular responses. As Christianity
came in, and the eating of horse-flesh was forbidden
as impiety by the Church, while his oracles dwindled
down to such as that which Falada's dead head
gives to the goose girl in the German tale, the
magic powers of the horse figured only in ballads
and legends: but his real power remained.

The art of riding became an hereditary and

exclusive science—at last a pedantry, hampered by
absurd etiquettes, and worse than useless traditions;
but the power and right to ride remained on the
whole the mark of the dominant caste. Terribly
did they often abuse that special power. The
faculty of making a horse carry him no more
makes a man a good man, than the faculties of
making money, making speeches, making books,
or making a noise about public abuses. And
of all ruffians, the worst, if history is to be
trusted, is the ruffian on a horse; to whose
brutality of mind is superadded the brute power
of his beast. A ruffian on a horse—what is there
that he will not ride over, and ride on, careless
and proud of his own shame? When the ancient
chivalry of France descended to that level, or rather
delegated their functions to mercenaries of that
level—when the knightly hosts who fought before
Jerusalem allowed themselves to be superseded by
the dragoons and dragonnades of Louis the Four-
teenth—then the end of the French chivalry was at
hand, and came. But centuries before that shameful
fall there had come in with Christianity the new

thought, that domination meant responsibility ;
that responsibility demanded virtue. The words
which denoted rank, came to denote likewise high
moral excellencies. The nobilis, or man who was
known, and therefore subject to public opinion,
was bound to behave nobly. The gentleman—
gentile-man — who respected his own gens, or
family and pedigree, was bound to be gentle. The
courtier, who had picked up at court some touch
of Roman civilization from Roman ecclesiastics,
was bound to be courteous. He who held an
" honour " or " edel " of land was bound to be
honourable ; and he who held a "weorthig," or
worthy, thereof, was bound himself to be worthy.
In like wise, he who had the right to ride a horse, was
expected to be chivalrous in all matters befitting the
hereditary ruler, who owed a sacred debt to a long
line of forefathers, as well as to the state in which
he dwelt ; all dignity, courtesy, purity, self-restraint,
devotion—such as they were understood in those
rough days—centred themselves round the idea of
the rider as the attributes of the man whose supposed duty, as well as his supposed right, was to

govern his fellow-men, by example, as well as by law
and force; — attributes which gathered themselves
up into that one word—Chivalry: an idea, which,
perfect or imperfect, God forbid that mankind
should ever forget, till it has become the possession
—as it is the God-given right—of the poorest slave
that ever trudged on foot; and every collier-lad
shall have become — as some of those Barnsley
men proved but the other day they had become
already—

"A very gentle perfect knight."

Very unfaithful was chivalry to its ideal—as all
men are to all ideals. But bear in mind, that if
the horse was the symbol of the ruling caste, it was
not at first its only strength. Unless that caste
had had at first spiritual, as well as physical force
on its side, it would have been soon destroyed—
nay, it would have destroyed itself—by internecine
civil war. And we must believe that those Franks,
Goths, Lombards, and Burgunds, who in the early
Middle Age leaped on the backs (to use Mr.
Carlyle's expression) of the Roman nations, were

actually, in all senses of the word, better men than
those whom they conquered. We must believe
it from reason; for if not, how could they, nu-
merically few, have held for a year, much more for
centuries, against millions, their dangerous elevation ?   We must believe it, unless we take Tacitus's
' Germania,' which I absolutely refuse to do, for a
romance. We must believe that they were better
than the Romanized nations whom they conquered,
because the writers of those nations, Augustine,
Salvian, and Sidonius Apollinaris, for example, say
that they were such, and give proof thereof. Not
good men according to our higher standard—far
from it ;   though Sidonius' picture of Theodoric,
the East Goth, in his palace of Narbonne, is
the picture of an eminently good and wise
ruler.   But not good, I say, as a rule—the Franks,
alas ! often very bad men : but still better, wiser,
abler, than those whom they ruled. We must
believe, too, that they were better, in every sense of
the word, than those tribes on their eastern frontier,
whom they conquered in after centuries, unless we
discredit (which we have no reason to do) the

accounts which the Roman and Greek writers give
of the horrible savagery of those tribes.

So·it was in later centuries. One cannot read
fairly the history of the Middle Ages without seeing that the robber knight of Germany or of France,
who figures so much in modern novels, must have
been the exception, and not the rule : that an
aristocracy which lived by the saddle would have
as little chance of perpetuating itself, as a priesthood composed of hypocrites and profligates ; that
the mediæval Nobility has been as much slandered
as the mediæval Church ; and the exceptions taken
—as more salient and exciting—for the average :
that side by side with ruffians like Gaston de Foix
hundreds of honest gentlemen were trying to do
their duty to the best of their light, and were
raising, and not depressing, the masses below them
—one very important item in that duty being, the
doing the whole fighting of the country at their
own expense, instead of leaving it to a standing
army of mercenaries, at the beck and call of a
despot ; and that, as M. De Tocqueville says, "In
feudal times, the Nobility were regarded pretty

much as the government is regarded in our own; the burdens they imposed were endured in consequence of the security they afforded. The nobles had many irksome privileges; they possessed many onerous rights: but they maintained public order, they administered justice, they caused the law to be executed, they came to the relief of the weak, they conducted the business of the community. In proportion as they ceased to do these things, the burden of their privileges appeared more oppressive, and their existence became an anomaly in proportion as they ceased to do these things." And the Ancien Regime may be defined as the period in which they ceased to do these things,—in which they began to play the idlers, and expected to take their old wages without doing their old work.

But in any case, government by a ruling caste, whether of the patriarchal or of the feudal kind, is no ideal or permanent state of society. So far from it, it is but the first or second step out of primæval savagery. For the more a ruling race becomes conscious of its own duty, and not merely of its own power—the more it learns to regard its peculiar gifts as entrusted to it for the good of men—so much the more earnestly will it labour to raise the masses below to its own level, by imparting to them its own light ; and so will it continually tend to abolish itself, by producing a general equality, moral and intellectual; and fulfil that law of self-sacrifice which is the beginning and the end of all virtue.

A race of noblest men and women, trying to make all below them as noble as themselves—that is at least a fair ideal, tending toward, though it has not reached, the highest ideal of all.

But suppose that the very opposite tendency —inherent in the heart of every child of man— should conquer. Suppose the ruling caste no longer the physical, intellectual, and moral superiors of the mass, but their equals. Suppose them—shameful, but not without example—actually sunk to be their inferiors. And that such a fall did come—nay, that it must have come—is matter of history. And its cause, like all social causes, was not a political, nor a physical, but a moral cause. The profligacy of the French and Italian aristocracies, in the sixteenth century, avenged itself on them by a curse (derived from the newly discovered America) from which they never recovered. The Spanish aristocracy suffered, I doubt not, very severely. The English and German, owing to the superior homeliness and purity of ruling their lives, hardly at all. But the continental caste, instead of recruiting their tainted blood by healthy blood from below, did all, under pretence of keeping it pure, to keep it tainted by continual intermarriage ; and paid, in increasing weakness of body and mind, the penalty of their exclusive pride. It is impossible for any one who reads the French memoirs of the sixteenth and seventeenth centuries, not to perceive, if he be wise, that the aristocracy therein depicted was ripe for ruin—yea, already ruined—under any form of government whatsoever, independent of all political changes. Indeed, many of the political changes were not the causes, but the effects, of the demoralization of the noblesse. Historians will tell you how, as early as the beginning of the seventeenth century, Henry IV. complained that the

nobles were quitting their country districts ; how
succeeding kings and statesmen, notably Richelieu
and Louis XIV, tempted the noblesse up to Paris,
that they might become mere courtiers, instead of
powerful country gentlemen ; how those who remained behind were only the poor hobereaux, little
hobby-hawks among the gentry, who considered it
degradation to help in governing the parish, as their
forefathers had governed it, and lived shabbily in
their chateaux, grinding the last farthing out of
their tenants, that they might spend it in town
during the winter. No wonder that with such an
aristocracy, who had renounced that very duty of
governing the country, for which alone they and
their forefathers had existed, there arose government
by intendants and sub-delegates, and all the other
evils of administrative centralization, which M. de
Tocqueville anatomizes and deplores. But what was
the cause of the curse? Their moral degradation.
What drew them up to Paris, save vanity and profligacy? What kept them from intermarrying with
the middle class, save pride? What made them
give up the office of governors, save idleness?

And if vanity, profligacy, pride, and idleness be .
not injustices and moral vices, what are ?

The race of heroic knights and nobles who
fought under the walls of Jerusalem—who wrestled,
and not in vain, for centuries with the equally
heroic English, in defence of their native soil—
who had set to all Europe the example of all
knightly virtues, had rotted down to this; their
only virtue left, as Mr. Carlyle says, being — a
perfect readiness to fight duels.

Every Intendant, chosen by the Comptroller-
General out of the lower-born members of the
Council of State; a needy young plebeian with his
fortune to make, and a stranger to the province, was,
in spite of his greed, ambition, chicane, arbitrary
tyranny, a better man—abler, more energetic, and
often, to judge from the pages of De Tocqueville,
with far more sympathy and mercy for the
wretched peasantry — than was the Count or
Marquis in the chateau above, who looked down
on him as a roturier; and let him nevertheless
become first his deputy, and then his master.

Understand me,—I am not speaking against the

hereditary principle of the Ancien Regime, but against its caste principle—two widely different elements, continually confounded now-a-days.

The hereditary principle is good, because it is founded on fact and nature. If men's minds come into the world blank sheets of paper — which I much doubt—every other part and faculty of them comes in stamped with hereditary tendencies and peculiarities. There are such things as transmitted capabilities for good and for evil ; and as surely as the offspring of a good horse or dog is likely to be good, so is the offspring of a good man, and still more of a good woman. If the parents have any special ability, their children will probably inherit it, at least in part ; and over and above, will have it developed in them by an education worthy of their parents and themselves. If man were—what he is not—a healthy and normal species, a permanent hereditary caste might go on intermarrying, and so perpetuate itself. But the same moral reason which would make such a caste dangerous—indeed, fatal to the liberty and development of mankind, make it happily

impossible. Crimes and follies are certain, after
a few generations, to weaken the powers of any
human caste; and unless it supplements its own
weakness by mingling again with the common
stock of humanity, it must sink under that weakness, as the ancient noblesse sank by its own vice.
Of course there were exceptions. The French
Revolution brought those exceptions out into
strong light; and like every day of judgment,
divided between the good and the evil. But it lies
not in exceptions to save a caste, or an institution ;
and a few Richelieus, Liancourts, Rochefoucaulds,
Noailles, Lafayettes were but the storks among
the cranes, involved in the wholesale doom due
not to each individual, but to a system and a class.

Profligacy, pride, idleness—these are the vices
which we have to lay to the charge of the Teutonic Nobility of the Ancien Regime in France
especially ; and (though in a less degree perhaps)
over the whole continent of Europe. But below
them, and perhaps the cause of them all, lay another and deeper vice—godlessness—atheism.

I do not mean merely want of religion, doc-

trinal unbelief. I mean want of belief in duty,
in responsibility. Want of belief that there was
a living God governing the universe, who had set
them their work, and would judge them according to their work. And therefore, want of belief,
yea, utter unconsciousness, that they were set in
their places to make the masses below them better
men; to impart to them their own civilization, to
raise them to their own level. They would have
shrunk from that which I just now defined as the
true duty of an aristocracy, just because it would
have seemed to them madness to abolish themselves. But the process of abolition went on,
nevertheless, only now from without instead of
from within. So it must always be, in such a case.
If a ruling class will not try to raise the masses
to their own level, the masses will try to drag
them down to theirs. That sense of justice which
allowed privileges, when they were as strictly official privileges as the salary of a judge, or the
immunity of a member of the House of Com-
mons; when they were earned, as in the Middle
Age, by severe education, earnest labour, and life

and death responsibility in peace and war, will demand the abolition of those privileges, when no work is done in return for them, with a voice which must be heard, for it is the voice of truth and justice.

But with that righteous voice will mingle another, most wicked, and yet, alas! most flattering to poor humanity—the voice of envy, simple and undisguised; of envy, which moralists hold to be one of the basest of human passions; which can never be justified, however hateful or unworthy be the envied man. And when a whole people, or even a majority thereof, shall be possessed by that, what is there that they will not do?

Some are surprised and puzzled when they find in the French Revolution of 1793, the noblest and the foulest characters labouring in concert, and side by side—often, too, paradoxical as it may seem, united in the same personage. The explanation is simple. Justice inspired the one; the other was the child of simple envy. But this passion of envy, if it becomes permanent and popular, may avenge itself, like all other sins. A nation may .

say to itself, " Provided we have no superiors to fall
our pride, we are content. Liberty is a slight
matter, provided we have equality. Let us be
slaves, provided we are all slaves alike." It may
destroy every standard of humanity above its
own mean average; it may forget that the old
ruling class, in spite of all its defects and crimes,
did at least pretend to represent something higher
than man's necessary wants, plus the greed of
amassing money; never meeting (at least in the
country districts) any one wiser or more refined
than an official or a priest drawn from the peasant
class, it may lose the belief that any standard
higher than that is needed ; and, all but forgetting
the very existence of civilization, sink contented
into a dead level of intellectual mediocrity and
moral barbarism, crying, " Let us eat and drink, for
to-morrow we die."

A nation in such a temper will surely be taken
at its word. Where the carcase is, there the eagles
will be gathered together; and there will not be
wanting to such nations—as there were not wanting in old Greece and Rome—despots who will

D 2

give them all they want, and more, and say to
them, "Yes, you shall eat and drink; and yet
you shall not die. For I, while I take care of your
mortal bodies, will see that care is taken of your
immortal souls."

For there are those who have discovered, with
the kings of the old Holy Alliance, that infidelity
and scepticism are political mistakes, not so much
because they promote vice, as because they promote (or are supposed to promote) free thought;
who see that religion (no matter of what quality)
is a most valuable assistant to the duties of a
minister of police. They will quote in their own
behalf Montesquieu's opinion that religion is a
column necessary to sustain the social edifice;
they will quote, too, that sound and true saying of
De Tocqueville's*—"If the first American who
might be met, either in his own country, or abroad,
were to be stopped and asked whether he considered religion useful to the stability of the laws
and the good order of society, he would answer,

* Mr. H. Reeves's translation of De Tocqueville's " France before the Revolution of 1789," p. 280.

without hesitation, that no civilized society, but
more especially none in a state of freedom, can
exist without religion. Respect for religion is, in
his eyes, the greatest guarantee of the stability of
the State, and of the safety of the community.
Those who are ignorant of the science of government, know that fact at least."

M. De Tocqueville, when he wrote these words,
was lamenting that in France, "freedom was for-
saken;" "a thing for which it is said that no one
any longer cares in France." He did not, it seems
to me, perceive that, as in America the best
guarantee of freedom is the reverence for a religion
or religions, which are free themselves, and which
teach men to be free; so in other countries the best
guarantee of slavery is, reverence for religions
which are not free, and which teach men to be
slaves.

But what M. De Tocqueville did not see, there
are others who will see; who will say—"If religion
be the pillar of political and social order, there is
an order which is best supported by a religion
which is adverse to free thought, free speech, free

conscience, free communion between man and God. The more enervating the superstition, the more exacting and tyrannous its priesthood, the more it will do our work, if we help it to do its own. If it permit us to enslave the body, we will permit it to enslave the soul."

And so may be inaugurated a period of that organized anarchy of which the poet says,

"It is not life, but death, when nothing stirs."

LECTURE II.

CENTRALIZATION.

THE degradation of the European nobility caused, of course, the increase of the kingly power, and opened the way to central despotisms. The bourgeoise, the commercial middle class, whatever were its virtues, its value, its real courage, were never able to stand alone against the kings. Their capital, being invested in trade, was necessarily subject to such sudden dangers from war, political change, bad seasons, and so forth, that its holders, however individually brave, were timid as a class. They could never hold out on strike against the governments, and had to submit to the powers that were, whatever they were, under penalty of ruin.

But on the Continent, and especially in France and Germany, unable to strengthen itself by

intermarriage with the noblesse, they retained
that timidity which is the fruit of the insecurity
of trade; and had to submit to a more and more
centralized despotism, and grow up as they could,
in the face of exasperating hindrances, to wealth,
to education, to the possession, in many parts of
France, of large landed estates; leaving the noblesse
to decay in isolated uselessness and weakness, and
in many cases debt and poverty.

The system—or rather anarchy—according to
which France was governed during this trans-
itional period, may be read in that work of M. De
Tocqueville's which I have already quoted, and
which is accessible to all classes, through Mr. H.
Reeves's excellent translation. Every student of
history is, of course, well acquainted with that
book. But as there is reason to fear, from language which is becoming once more too common,
both in speech and writing, that the general public
either do not know it, or have not understood it,
I shall take the liberty of quoting from it somewhat largely. I am justified in so doing by the
fact, that M. De Tocqueville's book is founded on

researches into the French Archives, which have
been made (as far as I am aware) only by him ;
and contains innumerable significant facts, which
are to be found (as far as I am aware) in no other
accessible work.

The French people (says M. De Tocqueville),
made, in 1789, the greatest effort which was ever
made by any nation to cut, so to speak, their
destiny in halves, and to separate by an abyss that
which they had heretofore been, from that which
they sought to become hereafter. But he had long
thought that they had succeeded in this singular
attempt much less than was supposed abroad ; and
less than they had at first supposed themselves.
He was convinced that they had unconsciously
retained, from the former state of society, most of
the sentiments, the habits, and even the opinions,
by means of which they had effected the destruc-
tion of that state of things; and that without intending it, they had used its remains to rebuild
the edifice of modern society. This is his thesis,
and this he proves, it seems to me, incontestably
by documentary evidence. Not only does he find

habits which we suppose—or supposed till lately
—to have died with the eighteenth century, still
living and working, at least in France, in the
nineteenth, but the new opinions which we look
on usually as the special children of the nineteenth century, he shows to have been born in the
eighteenth. France, he considers, is still at heart
what the Ancien Regime made her.

He shows that the hatred of the ruling caste, the
intense determination to gain and keep equality,
even at the expense of liberty, had been long growing up, under those influences of which I spoke in
my first lecture.

He shows, moreover, that the acquiescence in a
centralized administration ; the expectation that the
Government should do everything for the people,
and nothing for themselves ; the consequent loss of
local liberties, local peculiarities ; the helplessness
of the towns and the parishes ; and all which issued
in making Paris France, and subjecting the whole of
a vast country to the arbitrary dictates of a knot of
despots in the capital, was not the fruit of the Revolution, but of the Ancien Regime which preceded

it ;—and that Robespierre and his 'Comité de Salut Public,' and commissioners sent forth to the four winds of heaven in bonnet rouge and carmagnole complete, to build up and pull down, according to their wicked will, were only handling, somewhat more roughly, the same wires which had been handled for several generations past by the Comptroller-General and Council of State, with their provincial intendants.

"Do you know," said Law to the Marquis d'Argenson, "that this kingdom of France is governed by thirty intendants? You have neither parliament, nor estates, nor governors. It is upon thirty masters of requests, despatched into the provinces, that their evil or their good, their fertility or their sterility, entirely depend."

To do everything for the people, and let them do nothing for themselves—this was the Ancien Regime. To be more wise and more loving than Almighty God, who certainly does not do everything for the sons of men, but forces them to labour for themselves by bitter need, and after a most Spartan mode of education ; who allows them to burn their

hands as often as they are foolish enough to put
them into the fire; and to be filled with the fruits
of their own folly, even though the folly be one of
necessary ignorance; treating them with that seem-
ing neglect which is after all the most provident
care, because by it alone can men be trained to
experience, self help, science, true humanity; and
so become not tolerably harmless dolls, but men
and women worthy of the name; with

> " The reason firm, the temperate will,
> Endurance, foresight, strength, and skill ;
> The perfect spirit, nobly planned
> To cheer, to counsel, and command."

Such seems to be the education and government
appointed for man by the voluntatem Dei in rebus
revelatam, and the education, therefore, which the
man of science will accept and carry out. But the
men of the Ancien Regime—in as far as it was a
regime at all—tried to be wiser than the Almighty.
Why not? They were not the first, nor will be the
last, by many who have made the same attempt.
So this Council of State settled arbitrarily, not
only taxes and militia and roads, but anything

and everything. Its members meddled, with their whole hearts and minds. They tried to teach agriculture by schools and pamphlets and prizes; they sent out plans for every public work. A town could not establish an octroi, levy a rate, mortgage, sell, sue, farm, or administer their property, without an order in council. The Government ordered public rejoicings, saw to the firing of salutes, and illuminating of houses—in one case mentioned by M. De Tocqueville, they fined a member of the burgher guard for absenting himself from a Te Deum. All self-government was gone. A country parish was, says Turgot, nothing but "an assemblage of cabins, and of inhabitants as passive as the cabins they dwelt in. Without an order of council, the parish could not mend the steeple after a storm, or repair the parsonage gable. If they grumbled at the intendant, he threw some of the chief persons into prison, and made the parish pay the expenses of the horse patrol, which formed the arbitrary police of France. Everywhere was meddling. There were reports on statistics—circumstantial, inaccurate, and useless—as statistics

are too often wont to be. Sometimes, when the
people were starving, the Government sent down
charitable donations to certain parishes, on condition that the inhabitants should raise a sum on
their part. When the sum offered was sufficient,
the Comptroller-General wrote on the margin, when
he returned the report to the intendant, "Good—
express satisfaction." If it was more than sufficient, he wrote, "Good—express satisfaction and
sensibility." There is nothing new under the sun.
In 1761, the Government, jealous enough of news-
papers, determined to start one for itself, and for
that purpose took under its tutelage the Gazette
de France. So the public newsmongers were of
course to be the provincial intendants, and their
sub-newsmongers, of course, the sub-delegates.

But alas! the poor sub-delegates seem to have
found either very little news, or very little which it
was politic to publish. One reports that a smuggler
of salt has been hung, and has displayed great
courage; another that a woman in his district has
had three girls at a birth; another that a dreadful
storm has happened, but—has done no mischief;

a fourth—living in some specially favoured Utopia
—declares that in spite of all his efforts he has
found nothing worth recording, but that he himself
will subscribe to so useful a journal, and will exhort
all respectable persons to follow his example : in
spite of which loyal endeavours, the journal seems to
have proved a failure, to the great disgust of the
king and his minister, who had of course expected
to secure fine weather by nailing, like the school-
boy before a holiday, the hand of the weather-
glass.

Well had it been, if the intermeddling of this
bureaucracy had stopped there. But, by a process of evocation (as it was called), more and more
causes, criminal as well as civil, were withdrawn
from the regular tribunals, to those of the intendants and the Council. Before the intendant all
the lower order of people were generally sent for
trial. Bread-riots were a common cause of such
trials, and M. De Tocqueville asserts that he has
found sentences, delivered by the intendant, and
a local council chosen by himself, by which men
were condemned to the galleys, and even to death.

Under such a system, under which an intendant must have felt it his interest to pretend, at all risks, that all was going right, and to regard any disturbance as a dangerous exposure of himself and his chiefs—one can understand easily enough that scene which Mr. Carlyle has dramatized from Lacretelle, concerning the canaille, the masses, as we used to call them a generation since :—

"A dumb generation—their voice only an inarticulate cry. Spokesman, in the king's council, in the world's forum, they have none that finds credence. At rare intervals (as now, in 1775) they will fling down their hoes and, hammers; and, to the astonishment of mankind, flock hither and thither, dangerous, aimless, get the length even of Versailles. Turgot is altering the corn trade, abrogating the absurdest corn laws ; there is dearth, real, or were it even factitious, an indubitable scarcity of bread. And so, on the 2d day of May, 1775, these waste multitudes do here, at Versailles chateau, in wide-spread wretchedness, in sallow faces, squalor, winged raggedness, present as in legible hieroglyphic writing their petition of grievances. The chateau gates must be shut; but the king will appear on the balcony and speak to them. They have seen the king's face; their petition of grievances has been, if not read, looked at. In answer, two of them are hanged, " on a new gallows forty feet high, and the rest driven back to their dens for a time."

Of course. What more exasperating and inexpiable insult to the ruling powers was possible than this? To persist in being needy and wretched, when a whole bureaucracy is toiling day and night to make them prosperous and happy? An insult only to be avenged in blood. Remark meanwhile, that this centralized bureaucracy was a failure; that after all the trouble taken to govern these masses, they were not governed, in the sense of being made better, and not worse. The truth is, that no centralized bureaucracy, or so-called " paternal government," yet invented on earth, has been anything but a failure, or is like to be anything else: because it is founded on an error; because it regards and treats men as that which they are not, as things; and

E

not as that which they are, as persons. If the bureaucracy were a mere Briareus giant, with a hundred hands, helping the weak throughout the length and breadth of the empire, the system might be at least tolerable. But what if the Government were not a Briareus with a hundred hands, but a Hydra with a hundred heads and mouths, each far more intent on helping itself than on helping the people? What if sub-delegates and other officials, holding office at the will of the intendant, had to live, and even provide against a rainy day? What if intendants, holding office at the will of the Comptroller-General, had to do more than live, and found it prudent to realize as large a fortune as possible, not only against disgrace, but against success, and the dignity fit for a new member of the Noblesse de la Robe? Would not the system, then, soon become intolerable? Would there not be evil times for the masses, till they became something more than masses?

It is an ugly name, that of " The Masses," for the great majority of human beings in a nation. He who uses it speaks of them not as human beings, but as things; and as things not bound together in one living body, but lying in a fortuitous heap. A swarm of ants is not a mass. It has a polity and a unity. Not the ants, but the fir-needles and sticks, of which the ants have piled their nest, are a mass.

The term, I believe, was invented during the Ancien Regime. Whether it was or not, it expresses very accurately the life of the many in those days. No one would speak, if he wished to speak exactly, of the masses of the United States; for there every man is, or is presumed to be, a personage; with his own independence, his own activities, his own rights and duties. No one, I believe, would have talked of the masses in the old feudal times; for then each individual was some one's man, bound to his master by ties of mutual service, just or unjust, honourable or base, but still giving him a personality of duties and rights, and dividing him from his class.

Dividing, I say. The poor of the middle age had little sense of a common humanity. Those who owned allegiance to the lord in the next valley

were not their brothers ; and at their own lord's
bidding, they buckled on sword and slew the next
lord's men, with joyful heart and good conscience.
Only now and then misery compressed them into
masses; and they ran together, as sheep run together
to face a dog. Some wholesale wrong made them '
aware that they were brothers, at least in the power
of starving ; and they joined in the cry which was
heard, I believe, in Mecklenburg as late as 1790—
" Den Edelman wille wi dodschlagen." Then, in
Wat Tyler's insurrections, in Munster Anabaptisms,
in Jacqueries, they proved themselves to be masses,
if nothing better, striking for a while, by the mere
weight of numbers, blows terrible, though aimless
—soon to be dispersed and slain in their turn
by a disciplined and compact aristocracy. Yet
not always dispersed, if they could find a leader ;
as the Polish nobles discovered to their cost in the
middle of the seventeenth century. Then Bogdan
the Cossack, a wild warrior, not without his sins,
but having deserved well of James Sobieski and
the Poles, found that the neighbouring noble's
steward had taken a fancy to his windmill and his

farm upon the Dnieper. He was thrown into prison on a frivolous charge, and escaped to the Tatars, leaving his wife dishonoured, his house burnt, his infant lost in the flames, his eldest son scourged for protesting against the wrong. And he returned, at the head of an army of Tatars, Socinians, Greeks, or what not, to set free the serfs, and exterminate Jesuits, Jews, and nobles, throughout Podolia, Volhynia, Red Russia ; to desecrate the altars of God, and slay his servants ; to destroy the nobles by lingering tortures ; to strip noble ladies and maidens, and hunt them to death with the whips of his Cossacks ; and after defeating the nobles in battle after battle, to inaugurate an era of misery and anarchy from which Poland never recovered.

Thus did the masses of Southern Poland discover, for one generation at least, that they were not many things, but one thing ; a class, capable of brotherhood and unity, though, alas ! only of such as belongs to a pack of wolves. But such outbursts as this were rare exceptions. In general, feudalism kept the people divided, and therefore helpless.

And as feudalism died out, and with it the personal
self-respect and loyalty which were engendered by
the old relations of master and servant, the division still remained ; and the people, in France
especially, became merely masses, a swarm of
incoherent and disorganized things intent on the
necessaries of daily bread, like mites crawling over
each other in a cheese.

Out of this mass were struggling upwards perpetually, all who had a little ambition, a little
scholarship, or a little money, endeavouring to
become members of the middle class by obtaining
a Government appointment. "A man," says M. De
Tocqueville, "endowed with some education and
small means, thought it not decorous to die without
having been a Government officer." "Every man,
according to his condition," says a contemporary
writer, "wants to be something by command of the
king."

It was not merely the "natural vanity " of which
M. De Tocqueville accuses his countrymen, which
stirred up in them this eagerness after place ; for
we see the same eagerness in other nations of the

Continent, who cannot be accused (as wholes) of
that weakness. The fact is, a Government place,
or a Government decoration, cross, ribbon, or
what not, is, in a country where self-government is
unknown or dead, the only method, save literary
fame, which is left to men in order to assert themselves either to themselves or to their fellow-men.

A British or American shopkeeper or farmer
asks nothing of his Government. He can, if he
chooses, be elected to some local office (generally
unsalaried), by the votes of his fellow-citizens. But
that is his right; and adds nothing to his respecta-
bility. The test of that latter, in a country where
all honest callings are equally honourable, is the
amount of money he can make; and a very sound
practical test that is, in a country where intellect
and capital are free. Beyond that, he is what he
is; and wishes to be no more, save what he can
make himself. He has his rights, guaranteed by
law and public opinion; and as long as he stands
within them, and (as he well phrases it) behaves
like a gentleman, he considers himself as good as
any man; and so he is. But under the bureau-

cratic regime of the Continent, if a man had not
"something by command of the king," he was
nothing ; and something he naturally wished to be,
even by means of a Government which he disliked
and despised. So in France, where innumerable
petty posts were regular articles of sale, any one,
it seems, who had saved a little money, found it
most profitable to invest it in a beadledom of
some kind—to the great detriment of the country,
for he thus withdrew his capital from trade : but
to his own clear gain, for he thereby purchased
some immunity from public burdens, and, as it
were, compounded once and for all for his taxes.
The petty German princes, it seems, followed the
example of France, and sold their little beadledoms
likewise : but even where offices were not sold, they
must be obtained, by any and every means, by every
one who desired not to be as other men were, and
to become Notables, as they were called in France ;
so he migrated from the country into the nearest
town, and became a member of some small body
—guild, town council, or what not, bodies which
were infinite in number.   In one small town M. De

Tocqueville discovers thirty-six such bodies, "separated from each other by diminutive privileges, the least honourable of which was still a mark of honour." Quarrelling perpetually with each other for precedence, despising and oppressing the very menu peuple from whom they had for the most part sprung, these innumerable small bodies, instead of uniting their class, only served to split it up more and more ; and when the Revolution broke them up, once and for all, with all other privileges whatsoever, no bond of union was left; and each man stood alone, proud of his " individuality " — his complete social isolation ; till he discovered that, in ridding himself of superiors, he had rid himself also of fellows; fulfilling, every man in his own person, the old fable of the bundle of sticks; and had to submit, under the Consulate and the Empire, to a tyranny to which the Ancien Regime was freedom itself.

For, in France at least, the Ancien Regime was no tyranny. The middle and upper classes had individual liberty—it may be, only too much; the liberty of disobeying a Government which they did not re-

spect. " However submissive the French may have
been before the Revolution to the will of the king,
one sort of obedience was altogether unknown to
them. They knew not what it was to bow before
an illegitimate and contested power—a power but
little honoured, frequently despised, but willingly
endured because it may be serviceable, or because
it may hurt. To that degrading form of servi-
tude they were ever strangers. The king inspired
them with feelings . . . . which have become in-
comprehensible to this generation. . . . . . They
loved him with the affection due to a father ; they
revered him with the respect due to God. In
submitting to the most arbitrary of his commands,
they yielded less to compulsion than to loyalty ;
and thus they frequently preserved great freedom
of mind, even in the most complete dependence.
This liberty, irregular, intermittent," says M. De
Tocqueville, "helped to form those vigorous characters, those proud and daring spirits, which were
to make the French Revolution at once the object
of the admiration and the terror of succeeding
generations."

This liberty—too much akin to anarchy, in which indeed it issued for awhile—seems to have asserted itself in continual petty resistance to officials whom they did not respect, and who, in their turn, were more than a little afraid of the very men out of whose ranks they had sprung.

The French Government—one may say, every Government on the Continent in those days—had the special weakness of all bureaucracies ; namely, that want of moral force which compels them to fall back at last on physical force, and transforms the ruler into a bully, and the soldier into a policeman and a gaoler. A Government of parvenus, uncertain of its own position, will be continually trying to assert itself to itself, by vexatious intermeddling and intruding pretensions ; and then, when it meets with the resistance of free and rational spirits, will either recoil in awkward cowardice, or fly into a passion, and appeal to the halter and the sword. Such a Government can never take itself for granted, because it knows that it is not taken for granted by the people. It never can possess the quiet assurance, the courteous dignity, without swagger, yet without hesitation, which belongs to hereditary legislators; by which term is to be understood, not merely kings, not merely noblemen, but every citizen of a free nation, however democratic, who has received from his forefathers the right, the duty, and the example of self-government.

Such was the political and social state of the Ancien Regime, not only in France, but if we are to trust (as we must trust) M. De Tocqueville, in almost every nation in Europe, except Britain.

And as for its moral state. We must look for that—if we have need, which happily all have not —in its lighter literature.

I shall not trouble you with criticisms on French memoirs—of which those of Madame de Sevigné are, on the whole, the most painful (as witness her comments on the Marquise de Brinvilliers' execution), because written by a woman better and more human than ordinary. Nor with 'Menagiana,' or other 'ana's—as vain and artificial as they are often foul; nor with novels and poems, long since deservedly forgotten. On the first perusal

of this lighter literature, you will be charmed
with the ease, grace, lightness with which everything is said. On the second, you will be somewhat cured of your admiration, as you perceive
how little there is to say. The head proves to be
nothing but a cunning mask, with no brains inside.
Especially is this true of a book, which I must beg
those who have read it already, to recollect. To
read it I recommend no human being. We may
consider it, as it was considered in its time, the
typical novel of the Ancien Regime. A picture
of Spanish society, written by a Frenchman, it was
held to be—and doubtless with reason—a picture
of the whole European world. Its French editor
(of 1836) calls it a grande épopée; "one of the
most prodigious efforts of intelligence, exhausting
all forms of humanity,"—in fact, a second Shake-
speare, according to the lights of the year 1715.
I mean, of course, 'Gil Blas.' So picturesque is the
book, that it has furnished inexhaustible motifs
to the draughtsman. So excellent is its workman-
ship, that the enthusiastic editor of 1836 tells us—
and doubtless he knows best—that it is the classic

model of the French tongue ; and that, as Le Sage "had embraced all that belonged to man in his composition, he dared to prescribe to himself to embrace the whole French language in his work." It has been the parent of a whole school of literature ; the Bible of tens of thousands, with admiring commentators in plenty ; on whose souls may God have mercy !

And no wonder. The book has a solid value, and will always have, not merely from its perfect art (according to its own measure and intention), but from its perfect truthfulness. It is the Ancien Regime itself. It set forth to the men thereof, themselves, without veil, or cowardly reticence of any kind ; and inasmuch as every man loves himself, the Ancien Regime loved Gil Blas, and said, " The problem of humanity is solved at last." But, ye long-suffering powers of heaven, what a solution ! It is beside the matter to call the book ungodly, immoral, base. Le Sage would have answered— " Of course it is ; for so is the world, of which it is a picture." No ; the most notable thing about the book is its intense stupidity ; its dreariness, barrenness, shallowness, ignorance of the human heart, want of any human interest. If it be an epos, the actors in it are not men and women, but ferrets —with here and there, of course, a stray rabbit, on whose brains they may feed. It is the inhuman mirror of an inhuman age, in which the healthy human heart can find no more interest than in a pathological museum.

That last, indeed, Gil Blas is; a collection of diseased specimens. No man or woman in the book, lay or clerical, gentle or simple, as far as I can remember, do their duty in any wise, even if they recollect that they have any duty to do. Greed, chicane, hypocrisy, uselessness, are the ruling laws of human society. A new Book of Ecclesiastes, crying, "Vanity of vanity, all is vanity;" the "conclusion of the whole matter" being left out, and the new Ecclesiastes rendered thereby diabolic, instead of like that old one, divine. For, instead of "Fear God and keep his commandments, for that is the whole duty of man," Le Sage sends forth the new conclusion, "Take care of thyself, and feed on thy neighbours, for

that is the whole duty of man." And very faithfully was his advice (easy enough to obey at all
times) obeyed for nearly a century after Gil
Blas appeared.

About the same time there appeared, by a remarkable coincidence, another work, like it the
child of the Ancien Regime, and yet as opposite to
it as light to darkness. If Le Sage drew men as
they were, Fenelon tried at least to draw them as
they might have been, and still might be, were they
governed by sages and by saints, according to the
laws of God. 'Télémaque' is an ideal—imperfect,
doubtless, as all ideals must be in a world in which
God's ways and thoughts are for ever higher than
man's: but an ideal nevertheless. If its construction is less complete than that of 'Gil Blas,' it is
because its aim is infinitely higher; because the
form has to be subordinated, here and there, to the
matter. If its political economy be imperfect,
often chimerical, it is because the mind of one man
must needs have been too weak to bring into shape
and order the chaos, social and economic, which he
saw around him. M. De Lamartine, in his brilliant

little Life of Fenelon, does not hesitate to trace
to the influence of 'Télémaque,' the Utopias which
produced the revolutions of 1793 and 1848. " The
saintly poet was," he says, "without knowing it, the
first Radical and the first communist of his century."
But it is something to have preached to princes
doctrines till then unknown, or at least forgotten
for many a generation; free trade, peace, inter-
national arbitration, and the "carrière ouverte aux
talents" for all ranks. It is something to have
warned his generation of the dangerous over-
growth of the metropolis; to have prophesied, as
an old Hebrew might have done, that the despotism which he saw around him would end in a
violent revolution. It is something to have combined the highest Christian morality with a hearty
appreciation of old Greek life; of its reverence for
bodily health and prowess; its joyous and simple
country society; its sacrificial feasts, dances, games;
its respect for the gods; its belief that they helped,
guided, inspired the sons of men. It is something
to have himself believed in God; in a living God,
who, both in this life and in all lives to come,

F

rewarded the good and punished the evil by inevitable laws. It is something to have warned a
young prince, in an age of doctrinal bigotry and
practical atheism, that a living God still existed,
and that his laws were still in force ; to have shown
him Tartarus crowded with the souls of wicked
monarchs, while a few of kingly race rested in
Elysium, and among them old pagans—Inachus,
Cecrops, Erichthon, Triptolemus, and Sesostris,
rewarded for ever for having done their duty,
each according to his light, to the flocks which
the gods had committed to their care. It is
something to have spoken to a prince, in such an
age, without servility, and without etiquette, of the
frailties and the dangers which beset arbitrary rulers;
to have told him that royalty "when assumed to
content oneself, is a monstrous tyranny ; when
assumed to fulfil its duties, and to conduct an innumerable people as a father conducts his children,
a crushing slavery, which demands an heroic courage
and patience."

Let us honour the courtier who dared speak
such truths ; and still more the saintly celibate who

had sufficient Catholicity of mind to envelope them in old Grecian dress, and, without playing false for a moment to his own Christianity, seek in the writings of heathen sages a wider and healthier view of humanity than was afforded by an ascetic creed.

No wonder that the appearance of 'Télémaque,' published in Holland without the permission of Fenelon, delighted throughout Europe that public which is always delighted with new truths, as long as it is not required to practise them. To read 'Télémaque' was the right and the enjoyment of every one. To obey it, the duty only of princes. No wonder that, on the other hand, this " Vengeance de peuples, leçon des rois," as M. de Lamartine calls it, was taken for the bitterest satire by Louis XIV., and completed the disgrace of one who had dared to teach the future king of France that he must show himself, in all things, the opposite of his grandfather. No wonder if Madame de Maintenon and the court looked on its portraits of wicked ministers and courtiers as caricatures of themselves; portraits too, which, " composed thus in the palace

F 2

of Versailles, under the auspices of that confidence
which the king had placed in the preceptor of his
heir, seemed a domestic treason." No wonder,
also, if the foolish and envious world outside was of
the same opinion; and after enjoying for a while
this exposure of the great ones of the earth, left
' Télémaque' as an Utopia with which private folks
had no concern; and betook themselves to the
easier and more practical model of 'Gil Blas.'

But there are solid defects in ' Télémaque'—
indicating corresponding defects in the author's
mind—which would have, in any case, prevented
its doing the good work which Fenelon desired;
defects which are natural, as it seems to me, to his
position as a Roman Catholic priest, however saintly
and pure, however humane and liberal. The king,
with him, is to be always the father of his people;
which is tantamount to saying, that the people are
to be always children, and in a condition of tutelage;
voluntary, if possible: if not, of tutelage still. Of
self-government, and education of human beings
into free manhood by the exercise of self-government, free will, free thought—of this Fenelon had

surely not a glimpse. A generation or two passed by, and then the peoples of Europe began to suspect that they were no longer children, but come to manhood ; and determined (after the example of Britain and of America) to assume the rights and duties of manhood, at whatever risk of excesses or mistakes : and then 'Télémaque' was relegated— half unjustly—as the slavish and childish dream of a past age, into the schoolroom, where it still remains.

But there is a defect in 'Télémaque,' which is perhaps deeper still. No woman in it exercises influence over man, except for evil. Minerva, the guiding and inspiring spirit, assumes of course as Mentor, a male form ; but her speech and thought is essentially masculine, and not feminine. Antiope is a mere lay-figure, introduced at the end of the book because Telemachus must needs be allowed to have hope of marrying some one or other. Venus plays but the same part as she does in the Tannenhauser legends of the Middle Age. Her hatred against Telemachus is an integral element of the plot. She, with the other women or nymphs of the romance, in spite of all Fenelon's mercy and courtesy toward human frailties, really rise no higher than the witches of the Malleus Maleficanum. Woman—as the old monk held who derived femina from fe, faith, and minus, less, because women have less faith than men—is, in 'Télémaque,' whenever she thinks or acts, the temptress, the enchantress; the victim (according to a very ancient calumny) of passions more violent, often more lawless, than man's.

Such a conception of woman must make 'Télémaque,' to the end of time, useless as a wholesome book of education. It must have crippled its influence, especially in France, in its own time. For there, for good and for evil, woman was asserting more and more her power, and her right to power, over the mind and heart of man. Rising from the long degradation of the Middle Ages, which had really respected her only when unsexed and celibate, the French woman had assumed, often lawlessly, always triumphantly, her just freedom; her true place as the equal, the coadjutor, the counsellor of man. Of all problems connected with the education of a young prince, that of the influence of woman was, in the France of the Ancien Regime, the most important And it was just that which Fenelon did not, perhaps dared not, try to touch ; and which he most certainly could not have solved. Meanwhile, not only Madame de Maintenon, but women whose names it were a shame to couple with hers, must have smiled at, while they hated, the saint who attempted to dispense not only with them, but with the ideal queen who should have been the helpmeet of the ideal king.

To those who believe that the world is governed by a living God, it may seem strange, at first sight, that this moral anarchy was allowed to endure ; that the avenging, and yet most purifying storm of the French Revolution, inevitable from Louis XIV.'s latter years, was not allowed to burst two generations sooner than it did. Is not the answer—that the question always is not of destroying the world, but of amending it ? And that amendment must always come from within, and not from without ? That men must be taught to become men, and mend their world themselves ? To educate men into self-

. government—that is the purpose of the government
of God ; and some of the men of the eighteenth
century did learn that lesson. As the century
rolled on, the human mind arose out of the slough
in which Le Sage found it, into manifold and beau-
tiful activity, increasing hatred of shams and lies,
increasing hunger after truth and usefulness. With
mistakes and confusions innumerable they worked :
but still they worked; planting good seed ; and when
the fire of the French Revolution swept over the
land, it burned up the rotten and the withered, only
to let the fresh herbage spring up from underneath.

But that purifying fire was needed. If we in-
quire why the many attempts to reform the Ancien
Regime, which the eighteenth century witnessed,
were failures one and all ; why Pombal failed in
Portugal, Aranda in Spain, Joseph II. in Austria,
Ferdinand and Caroline in Naples—for these last,
be it always remembered, began as humane and
enlightened sovereigns, patronizing liberal opinions,
and labouring to ameliorate the condition of the
poor, till they were driven by the murder of Marie
Antoinette into a paroxysm of rage and terror—

why, above all, Louis XVI. who attempted deeper and wiser reforms than any other sovereign, failed more disastrously than any—is not the answer this, that all these reforms would but have cleansed the outside of the cup and the platter, while they left the inside full of extortion and excess? It was not merely institutions which required to be reformed, but men and women. The spirit of Gil Blas had to be cast out. The deadness, selfishness, isolation of men's souls ; their unbelief in great duties, great common causes, great self-sacrifices —in a word, their unbelief in God, and themselves, and mankind—all that had to be reformed ; and till that was done all outward reform would but have left them, at best, in brute ease and peace, to that soulless degradation, which (as in the Byzantine empire of old, and seemingly in the Chinese empire of to-day) hides the reality of barbarism under a varnish of civilization. Men had to be awakened ; to be taught to think for themselves, act for themselves, to dare and suffer side by side for their country and for their children ; in a word, to arise and become men once more.

And what is more, men had to punish — to avenge. Those are fearful words. But there is, in this God-guided universe, a law of retribution, which will find men out, whether men choose to find it out or not: a law of retribution; of vengeance inflicted justly, though not necessarily by just men. The public executioner was seldom a very estimable personage, at least under the old Regime.; and those who have been the scourges of God have been, in general, mere scourges, and nothing better; smiting blindly, rashly, confusedly; confounding too often the innocent with the guilty, till they have seemed only to punish crime by crime, and replace old sins by new. But, however insoluble, however saddening that puzzle be, I must believe—as long as I believe in any God at all—that such men as Robespierre were his instruments, even in their crimes.

In the case of the French Revolution, indeed, the wickedness of certain of its leaders was part of the retribution itself. For the noblesse existed surely to make men better. It did, by certain classes, the very opposite. Therefore it was de-

stroyed by wicked men, whom it itself had made
wicked. For over and above all political, economic, social wrongs, there were wrongs personal,
human, dramatic; which stirred not merely the
springs of covetousness or envy, or even of a just
demand for the freedom of labour and enterprise :
but the very deepest springs of rage, contempt,
and hate ; wrongs which caused, as I believe, the
horrors of the Revolution.

It is notorious, how many of the men most
deeply implicated in those horrors were of the
artist class—by which I signify not merely painters
and sculptors—as the word artist has now got,
somewhat strangely, to signify, at least in England
—but what the French meant by artistes—pro-
ducers of luxuries and amusements, play-actors,
musicians, and suchlike, down to that "distracted
peruke-maker with two fiery torches," who at the
storm of the Bastile, "was for burning the salt-
petres of the Arsenal, had not a woman run scream-
ing; had not a patriot with some tincture of natural
philosophy, instantly struck the wind out of him,
with butt of musket on pit of stomach, overturned

the barrels, and stayed the devouring element."
The distracted peruke-maker may have had his
wrongs—perhaps such a one as that of poor Tri-
boulet the fool, in 'Le Roi s'amuse'—and his
own sound reasons for blowing down the Bastile,
and the system which kept it up.

For these very ministers of luxury—then miscalled art—from the periwig-maker to the play-
actor,—who like them had seen the frivolity, the
baseness, the profligacy, of the rulers to whose
vices they pandered, whom they despised while
they adored? Figaro himself may have looked up
to his master the Marquis as a superior being, as
long as the law enabled the Marquis to send him
to the Bastile by a lettre de cachet; yet Figaro
may have known and seen enough to excuse him,
when lettres de cachet were abolished, for hand-
ing the Marquis over to a Comité de Salut Public.
Disappointed play-actors, like Collet d'Herbois;
disappointed poets, like Fabre d'Olivet, were,
they say, especially ferocious. Why not? Inge-
nious, sensitive spirits, used as lap-dogs and sing-
ing-birds by men and women whom they felt to

be their own flesh and blood, they had, it may be, a juster appreciation of the actual worth of their patrons than had our own Pitt and Burke. They had played the valet: and no man was a hero to them. They had seen the nobleman expose himself before his own helots: they would try if the helot was not as good as the nobleman. The nobleman had played the mountebank: why should not the mountebank, for once, play the nobleman? The nobleman's God had been his five senses, with (to use Mr. Carlyle's phrase) the sixth sense of vanity: why should not the mountebank worship the same God, like Carrière at Nantes, and see what grace and gifts he too might obtain at that altar?

But why so cruel? Because, with many of these men, I more than suspect, there were wrongs to be avenged deeper than any wrongs done to the sixth sense of vanity. Wrongs common to them, and to a great portion of the respectable middle class, and much of the lower class: but wrongs to which they and their families, being most in contact with the noblesse, would be especially exposed; namely, wrongs to women.

Every one who knows the literature of that time, must know what I mean: what had gone on for more than a century, it may be more than two, in France, in Italy, and—I am sorry to have to say it—. Germany likewise. All historians know what ·I mean, and how enormous was the evil. I only wonder that they have so much overlooked that item in the causes of the Revolution. It seems to me to have been more patent. and potent in the sight of men, as it surely was in the sight of Almighty God, than all the political and economic wrongs put together. They might have issued in a change of dynasty or of laws. That, issued in the blood of the offenders. Not a girl was enticed into Louis the Fifteenth's Petit Trianon, or other den of aristocratic iniquity, but left behind her parents nursing shame and sullen indignation, even while they fingered the ill-gotten price of their daughter's honour; and left behind also, perhaps, some unhappy boy of her own class, in whom disappointment and jealousy were transformed—and who will blame him?—into righteous indignation, and a very sword of God; all the more indignant,

and all the more righteous, if education helped
him to see, that the maiden's acquiescence, her
pride in her own shame, was the ugliest feature
in the whole crime, and the most potent reason for
putting an end, however fearful, to a state of things
in which such a fate was thought an honour and
a gain, and not a disgrace and a ruin; in which
the most gifted daughters of the lower classes
had learnt to think it more noble to become—
that which they became—than the wives of honest
men.

If you will read fairly the literature of the
Ancien Regime, whether in France or elsewhere,
you will see that my facts are true. If you have
human hearts in you, you will see in them, it
seems to me, an explanation of many a guillo-
tinade and fusillade, as yet explained only on the
ground of madness—an hypothesis which (as we
do not yet in the least understand what madness
is) is no explanation at all.

An age of decay, incoherence, and makeshift,
varnish and gilding upon worm-eaten furniture, and
mouldering wainscot, was that same Ancien Regime.

And for that very reason a picturesque age; like one of its own landscapes. A picturesque bit of uncultivated mountain, swarming with the prince's game; a picturesque old robber schloss above, now in ruins; and below, perhaps, the picturesque new schloss, with its French fountains and gardens, French nymphs of marble, and of flesh and blood likewise, which the prince has partially paid for, by selling a few hundred young men to the English to fight the Yankees. The river, too, is picturesque, for the old bridge has not been repaired since it was blown up in the Seven Years' War; and there is but a single lazy barge floating down the stream, owing to the tolls and tariffs of his Serene Highness; the village is picturesque, for the flower of the young men are at the wars, and the place is tumbling down; and the two old peasants in the foreground, with the single goat and the hamper of vine-twigs, are very picturesque likewise, for they are all in rags.

How sad to see the picturesque element elimi-nated, and the quiet artistic beauty of the scene destroyed ;—to have steamers puffing up and down

the river, and a railroad hurrying along its banks
the wealth of the Old World, in exchange for the
wealth of the New—or hurrying, it may be, whole
regiments of free and educated citizen-soldiers, who
fight, they know for what. How sad to see the alte
schloss desecrated by tourists, and the neue schloss
converted into a cold-water cure. How sad to see
the village, church and all, built up again bran-new,
and whitewashed to the very steeple top;—a new
school at the town end—a new crucifix by the
wayside. How sad to see the old folk well clothed
in the fabrics of England or Belgium, doing an
easy trade in milk and fruit, because the land they
till has become their own, and not the prince's ;
while their sons are thriving farmers on the prairies
of the far West. Very unpicturesque, no doubt, is
wealth and progress, peace and safety, cleanliness
and comfort. But they possess advantages unknown to the Ancien Regime, which was, if nothing
else, picturesque. Men could paint amusing and
often pretty pictures of its people and its places.

Consider that word, picturesque. It, and the
notion of art which it expresses, are the children of

G

the Ancien Regime—of the era of decay. The
healthy, vigorous, earnest, progressive middle age
never dreamed of admiring, much less of painting,
for their own sake, rags and ruins; the fashion
sprang up at the end of the seventeenth century;
it lingered on during the first quarter of our century, kept alive by the reaction from 1815-25. It
is all but dead now, before the return of vigorous
and progressive thought. An admirer of the
middle ages now does not build a sham ruin
in his grounds; he restores a church, blazing
with colour, like a mediæval illumination. He
has learnt to look on that which went by the
name of picturesque in his great-grandfather's
time, as an old Greek or a middle age monk would
have done—as something squalid, ugly, a sign of
neglect, disease, death; and therefore to be hated
and abolished, if it cannot be restored. At Car-
cassone, now, M. Viollet-le-Duc, under the auspices
of the Emperor of the French, is spending his vast
learning, and much money, simply in abolishing
the picturesque; in restoring stone for stone, each
member of that wonderful museum of middle age

architecture: Roman, Visigothic, Moslem, Romaine,
Early English, later French, all is being reproduced
exactly as it must have existed centuries since.
No doubt that is not the highest function of art:
but it is a preparation for the highest, a step toward
some future creative school. As the early Italian
artists, by careful imitation, absorbed into their
minds the beauty and meaning of old Greek
and Roman art; so must the artists of our days by
the art of the middle age and the Renaissance.
They must learn to copy, before they can learn to
surpass; and, meanwhile, they must learn—indeed
they have learnt—that decay is ugliness, and the
imitation of decay, a making money out of the
public shame.

The picturesque sprang up, as far as I can discover, suddenly, during the time of exhaustion and
recklessness which followed the great struggles of
the sixteenth century. Salvator Rosa and Callot,
·two of the earliest professors of picturesque art,
have never been since surpassed. For, indeed, they
drew from life. The rags and the ruins, material,
and, alas spiritual, were all around them; the

G 2

lands and the creeds alike lay waste. There was ruffianism and misery among the masses of Europe; unbelief and artificiality among the upper classes; churches and monasteries defiled, cities sacked, farmsteads plundered and ruinate, and all the wretchedness which Callot has immortalized—for a warning to evil rulers—in his Misères de la Guerre. The world was all gone wrong: but as for setting it right again—who could do that? And so men fell into a sentimental regret for the past, and its beauties, all exaggerated by the foreshortening of time; while they wanted strength or faith to reproduce it. At last they became so accustomed to the rags and ruins, that they looked on them as the normal condition of humanity, as the normal field for painters.

Only now and then, and especially toward the latter half of the eighteenth century, when thought began to revive, and men dreamed of putting the world to rights once more, there rose before them glimpses of an Arcadian ideal. Country life—the primæval calling of man,—how graceful and pure it might be! How graceful—

if not pure—it once had been! The boors of
Teniers and the beggars of Murillo might be true
to present fact; but there was a fairer ideal, which
once had been fact, in the Eclogues of Theocritus,
and the Loves of Daphnis and Chloe. And so
men took to dreaming of shepherds and shepherdesses, and painting them on canvass, and
modelling them in china, according to their
cockney notions of what they had been once,
and always ought to be. We smile now at
Sèvres and Dresden shepherdesses; but the wise
man will surely see in them a certain pathos. They
indicated a craving after something better than
boorishness; and the many men and women
may have become the gentler and purer by
looking even at them, and have said sadly to
themselves—"Such might have been the peasantry
of half Europe, had it not been for devastations of
the Palatinate, wars of succession, and the wicked
wills of emperors and kings."

LECTURE III.

THE EXPLOSIVE FORCES.

IN a former lecture in this Institution, I said that the human race owed more to the eighteenth century, than to any century since the Christian era. It may seem a bold assertion, to those who value duly the century which followed the revival of Greek literature, and consider, that the eighteenth century was but the child, or rather grandchild, thereof. But I must persist in my opinion, even though it seem to be inconsistent with my description of the very same era as one of decay and death. For side by side with the death, there was manifold fresh birth; side by side with the decay there was active growth;—side by side with them, fostered by them, though generally in strong opposition to them, whether conscious or unconscious. We must beware, however, of trying to find be-

tween that decay and that growth a bond of
cause and effect where there is really none. The
general decay may have determined the course
of many men's thoughts ; but it no more set
them thinking than (as I have heard said) the
decay of the Ancien Regime produced the new Regime—a loose metaphor, which, like all metaphors,
will not hold water, and must not be taken for a
philosophic truth. That would be to confess man—
what I shall never confess him to be—the creature
of circumstances ; it would be to fall into the
same fallacy of spontaneous generation as did the
ancients, when they believed that bees were bred
from the carcase of a dead ox. In the first place,
the bees were no bees, but flies—unless when some
true swarm of honey bees may have taken up their
abode within the empty ribs, as Samson's bees did
in that of the lion. But bees or flies, each sprung
from an egg, independent of the carcass, having a
vitality of its own : it was fostered by the carcass
it fed on during development ; but bred from it
it was not, any more than Marat was bred from
the decay of the Ancien Regime. There are flies

which, by feeding on putridity, become poisonous
themselves, as did Marat : but even they owe their
vitality and organization to something higher than
that on which they feed ; and each of them, however, defaced and debased, was at first a " thought
of God." All true manhood consists in the defiance of circumstances ; and if any man be the
creature of circumstances, it is because he has
become so, like the drunkard ; because he has
ceased 'to be a man, and sunk downward toward
the brute.

Accordingly we shall find, throughout the eight-
teenth century, a stirring of thought, an originality,
a resistance to circumstances, an indignant defiance
of circumstances, which would have been impossible, had circumstances been the true lords and
shapers of mankind. Had that latter been the
case, the downward progress of the Ancien Regime
would have been irremediable. Each generation,
conformed more and more to the element in which
it lived, would have sunk deeper in dull acquiescence to evil, in ignorance of all cravings save those
of the senses ; and if at any time intolerable wrong

or want had driven it to revolt, it would have issued, not in the proclamation of new and vast ideas, but in an anarchic struggle for revenge and bread.

There are races, alas! which seem, for the present at least, mastered by circumstances. Some, like the Chinese, have sunk back into that state; some, like the negro in Africa, seem not yet to have emerged from it. But in Europe, during the eighteenth century, were working not merely new forces and vitalities (abstractions which mislead rather than explain), but living persons in plenty, men and women, with independent and original hearts and brains, instinct, in spite of all circumstances, with power which we shall most wisely ascribe directly to Him who is the Lord and Giver of Life.

Such persons seemed—I only say seemed—most numerous in England and in Germany. But there were enough of them in France to change the destiny of that great nation for awhile—perhaps for ever.

M. De Tocqueville has a whole chapter, and a

very remarkable one, which appears at first sight
to militate against my belief—a chapter "showing
that France was the country in which men had
become most alike."

"The men," he says, "of that time, especially
those belonging to the upper and middle ranks of
society, who alone were at all conspicuous, were
all exactly alike."

And it must be allowed, that if this were true
of the upper and middle classes, it must have been
still more true of the mass of the lowest population,
who, being most animal, are always most moulded
—or rather crushed—by their own circumstances,
by public opinion, and by the wants of five senses,
common to all alike.

But when M. De Tocqueville attributes this
curious fact to the circumstances of their political
state—to that "government of one man which in
the end has the inevitable effect of rendering all
men alike, and all mutually indifferent to their
common fate"—we must differ, even from him : for
facts prove the impotence of that, or of any other
circumstance, in altering the hearts and souls of

men, in producing in them anything but a mere superficial and temporary resemblance.

For all the while there was, among these very French, here and there a variety of character and purpose, sufficient to burst through that very despotism, and to develop the nation into manifold, new, and quite original shapes. Thus it was proved that the uniformity had been only in their outside crust and shelL What tore the nation to pieces during the Reign of Terror, but the boundless variety and originality of the characters which found themselves suddenly in free rivalry? What else gave to the undisciplined levies, the bankrupt governments, the parvenu heroes of the Republic, a manifold force, a self-dependent audacity, which made them the conquerors, and the teachers (for good and evil), of the civilized world? If there was one doctrine which the French Revolution specially proclaimed—which it caricatured till it brought it into temporary disrepute—it was this: that no man is like another; that in each is a God-given "individuality," an independent soul, which no government or man has a right to crush, or can

crush in the long run : but which ought to have, and
must have, a "carrière ouverte aux talents," freely
to do the best for itself in the battle of life. The
French Revolution, more than any event since
twelve poor men set forth to convert the world
some eighteen hundred years ago, proves that man
ought not to be, and need not be, the creature of
circumstances, the puppet of institutions; but, if
he will, their conqueror and their lord.

Of these original spirits, who helped to bring life
out of death, and the modern world out of the decay
of the mediæval world, the French "philosophes"
and encyclopædists are, of course, the most notorious. They confessed, for the most part, that
their original inspiration had come from England.
They were, or considered themselves, the disciples
of Locke; whose philosophy, it seems to me, their
own acts disproved.

And first, a few words on these same "philosophes." One may be thoroughly aware of their
deficiencies, of their sins, moral as well as intellectual : and yet one may demand that every
one should judge them fairly—which can only

be done by putting himself in their place; and any fair judgment of them will, I think, lead to the conclusion that they were not mere destroyers, inflamed with hate of everything which mankind had as yet held sacred. Whatever sacred things they despised, one sacred thing they reverenced, which men had forgotten more and more since the seventeenth century—common justice, and common humanity. It was this, I believe, which gave them their moral force. It was this which drew towards them the hearts, not merely of educated bourgeois and nobles (on the *menu peuple* they had no influence, and did not care to have any), but of every continental sovereign who felt in himself higher aspirations than those of a mere selfish tyrant—Frederick the Great, Christina of Sweden, Joseph of Austria, and even that fallen Juno, Catharine of Russia, with all her sins. To take the most extreme instance— Voltaire. We may question his being a philosopher at all. We may deny that he had even a tincture of formal philosophy. We may doubt much whether he had any of that human and humorous

common-sense, which is often a good substitute
for the philosophy of the schools. We may feel
against him a just and honest indignation when we
remember that he dared to travestie into a foul
satire, the tale of his country's purest and noblest
heroine ; but we must recollect, at the same time,
that he did a public service to the morality of his
own country, and of all Europe, by his indignation—quite as just and honest as any which we
may feel—at the legal murder of Calas. We must
recollect that, if he exposes baseness and foulness
with too cynical a licence of speech (in which,
indeed, he sinned no more than had the average
of French writers since the days of Montaigne),
he at least never advocates them, as did Le Sage.
We must recollect that, scattered throughout his
writings, are words in favour of that which is just,
merciful, magnanimous, and even, at times, in
favour of that which is pure; which proves that in
Voltaire, as in most men, there was a double self—
the one sickened to cynicism by the iniquity and
folly which he saw around him—the other, hunger-
ing after a nobler life, and possibly exciting that

hunger in one and another, here and there, who admired him for other reasons than the educated mob, which cried after him "Vive la Pucelle."

Rousseau, too. Easy it is to feel disgust, contempt, for the 'Confessions' and the 'Nouvelle Heloise'—for much, too much, in the man's own life and character. One would think the worse of the young Englishman who did not so feel, and express his feelings roundly and roughly. But all young Englishmen should recollect, that to Rousseau's 'Emile' they owe their deliverance from the useless pedantries, the degrading brutalities, of the mediæval system of school-education; that 'Emile' awakened throughout civilized Europe a conception of education just, humane, rational, truly scientific, because founded upon facts; that if it had not been written by one writhing under the bitter consequences of mis-education, and feeling their sting and their brand day by day on his own spirit, Miss Edgworth might never have reformed our nurseries, or Dr. Arnold our public schools.

And so with the rest of the "philosophes."

That there were charlatans among them, vain men, pretentious men, profligate men, selfish, self-seeking and hypocritical men, who doubts? Among what class of men were there not such in those evil days? In what class of men are there not such now, in spite of all social and moral improvement? But nothing but the conviction, among the average, that they were in the right—that they were fighting a battle for which it was worth while to dare, and if need be to suffer, could have enabled them to defy what was then public opinion, backed by overwhelming physical force.

Their intellectual defects are patent. No one can deny that their inductions were hasty and partial; but then they were inductions, as opposed to the dull pedantry of the schools, which rested on tradition only half-believed, or pretended to be believed. No one can deny that their theories were too general and abstract : but then they were theories as opposed to the no-theory of the Ancien Regime, which was, "Let us eat and drink, for to-morrow we die."

Theories—principles—by them if men do not live, by them men are, at least, stirred into life, at the sight of something more noble than themselves. Only by great ideas, right or wrong, could such a world as that which Le Sage painted, be roused out of its slough of foul self-satisfaction, and equally foul self-discontent.

For mankind is ruled and guided, in the long run, not by practical considerations, not by self-interest, not by compromises: but by theories and principles, and those of the most abstruse, delicate, supernatural, and literally unspeakable kind; which, whether they be according to reason or not, are so little according to logic—that is, to speakable reason—that they cannot be put into speech. Men act, whether singly or in masses, by impulses and instincts for which they give reasons quite incompetent, often quite irrelevant: but which they have caught from each other, as they catch fever or small-pox; as unconsciously, and yet as practically and potently: just as the nineteenth century has caught from the philosophers of the eighteenth, most practical rules of conduct

H

without even (in most cases) having read a word
of their works.

And what has this century caught from these
philosophers? One rule it has learnt, and that a
most practical one—to appeal in all cases, as
much as possible, to " Reason and the Laws of
Nature." That, at least, the philosophers tried
to do. Often they failed. Their conceptions of
reason and of the laws of nature being often
incorrect, they appealed to unreason, and to laws
which were not those of nature. " The fixed
idea of them all was," says M. De Tocqueville,
"to substitute simple and elementary rules, de-
duced from reason and natural law, for the complicated traditional customs which governed the
society of their time." They were often rash,
hasty, in the application of their method. They
ignored whole classes of facts, which, though
spiritual and not physical, are just as much facts,
and facts for science, as those which concern a stone
or a fungus. They mistook for merely complicated
traditional customs, many most sacred institutions
which were just as much founded on reason and

natural law, as any theories of their own. But who shall say that their method was not correct? That it was not the only method? They appealed to reason. Would you have had them appeal to unreason? They appealed to natural law. Would you have had them appeal to unnatural law?—law according to which God did not make this world? Alas! that had been done too often already. Solomon saw it done in his time, and called it folly, to which he prophesied no good end. Rabelais saw it done in his time; and wrote his chapters on the 'Children of Physis and the Children of Antiphysis.' But, born in an evil generation, which was already, even in 1500, ripening for the revolution of 1789, he was sensual and, I fear, cowardly enough to hide his light, not under a bushel, but under a dunghill; till men took him for a jester of jests; and his great wisdom was lost to the worse and more foolish generations which followed him, and thought they understood him.

But as for appealing to natural law for that which is good for men, and to reason for the power of discerning that same good—if man cannot find truth by that method, by what method shall he find it?

And thus it happened that, though these philosophers and encyclopædists were not men of science, they were at least the heralds and the coadjutors of science.

We may call them, and justly, dreamers, theorists, fanatics. But we must recollect that one thing they meant to do, and did. They recalled men to facts; they bid them ask of everything they saw—What are the facts of the case? Till we know the facts, argument is worse than useless.

Now the habit of asking for the facts of the case must deliver men more or less from that evil spirit which the old Romans called "Fama;" from her whom Virgil described in the Æneid as the ugliest, the falsest, and the cruellest of monsters.

From "Fama;" from rumours, hearsays, exaggerations, scandals, superstitions, public opinions—whether from the ancient public opinion that the sun went round the earth, or the equally public opinion, that those who dared to differ from public opinion were hateful to the deity, and therefore

worthy of death ;—from all these blasts of Fame's
lying trumpet they helped to deliver men ; and they
therefore helped to insure something like peace
and personal security for those quiet, modest,
and generally virtuous men, who, as students of
physical science, devoted their lives, during the
eighteenth century, to asking of nature—What are
the facts of the case ?

It was no coincidence, but a connexion of cause
and effect, that during the century of 'philosophes,'
sound physical science throve, as she had never
thriven before; that in zoology and botany, chemis-
try and medicine, geology and astronomy, man after
man, both of the middle and the noble classes, laid
down on more and more sound, because more and
more extended foundations, that physical science
which will endure as an everlasting heritage to
mankind ; endure, even though a second Byzantine
period should reduce it to a timid and traditional
pedantry, or a second irruption of barbarians sweep
it away for a while, to revive again (as classic philosophy revived in the fifteenth century) among new
and more energetic races; when the kingdom of

God shall have been taken away from us, and given to a nation bringing forth the fruits thereof.

An eternal heritage, I say, for the human race; which once gained, can never be lost; which stands, and will stand, marches, and will march, proving its growth, its health, its progressive force, its certainty of final victory, by those very changes, disputes, mistakes, which the ignorant and the bigoted hold up to scorn, as proofs of its uncertainty and its rottenness; because they never have dared or cared to ask boldly—What are the facts of the case?—and have never discovered either the acuteness, the patience, the calm justice, necessary for ascertaining the facts, or their awful and divine certainty when once ascertained.

[But these philosophers (it will be said) hated all religion.

Before that question can be fairly discussed, it is surely right to consider what form of religion that was which they found working round them in France, and on the greater part of the Continent. The quality thereof may have surely had something to do (as they themselves asserted) with that "sort of rage" with which (to use M. De Tocqueville's words) "the Christian religion was attacked in France."

M. De Tocqueville is of opinion (and his opinion is likely to be just) that "the Church was not more open to attack in France than elsewhere; that the corruptions and abuses which had been allowed to creep into it were less, on the contrary, there than in most Catholic countries. The Church of France was infinitely more tolerant than it ever had been previously, and than it still was among other nations. Consequently, the peculiar causes of this phenomenon" (the hatred which it aroused) "must be looked for less in the condition of religion than in that of society."

"We no longer," he says, shortly after, "ask in what the Church of that day erred as a religious institution, but how far it stood opposed to the political revolution which was at hand." And he goes on to show how the principles of her ecclesiastical government, and her political position, were such that the philosophes must needs have been her enemies. But he mentions another fact which seems to me to belong neither to the category of religion nor to that of politics; a fact which, if he had done us the honour to enlarge upon it, might have led him and his readers to a more true understanding of the disrepute into which Christianity had fallen in France.

" The ecclesiastical authority had been specially employed in keeping watch over the progress of thought; and the censorship of books was a daily annoyance to the 'philosophes.' By defending the common liberties of the human mind against the Church, they were combating in their own cause : and they began by breaking the shackles which pressed most closely on themselves."

Just so. And they are not to be blamed if they pressed first and most earnestly reforms which they knew by painful experience to be necessary. All reformers are wont thus to begin at home. It is to their honour if, not content with shaking off their own fetters, they begin to see that others are fettered likewise ; and, reasoning from the particular to the universal, to learn that their own cause is the cause of mankind.

There is, therefore, no reason to doubt that these men were honest, when they said that they were combating, not in their own cause merely, but in that of humanity; and that the Church was combating in her own cause, and that of her power and privilege. The Church replied that she, too, was combating for humanity; for its moral and eternal well-being. But that is just what the 'philosophes' denied. They said (and it is but fair to take a statement which appears on the face of all their writings; which is the one key-note on which they ring perpetual changes), that the cause of the Church in France was not that of humanity, but of inhumanity; not that of nature, but of unnature; not even that of grace, but of disgrace. Truly or falsely, they complained that the French clergy had not only identified themselves with the repression of free thought, and of physical science, especially that of the Newtonian astronomy, but that they had proved themselves utterly unfit, for centuries past, to exercise any censorship whatsoever over the thoughts of men : that they had identified themselves with the cause of darkness, not of light ;

with persecution and torture, with the dragonnades of Louis XIV., with the murder of Calas and
of Urban Grandier ; with celibacy, hysteria, demon-
ology, witchcraft, and the shameful public scandals,
like those of Gauffredi, Grandier, and Père Giraud,
which had arisen out of mental disease ; with
forms of worship which seemed to them (rightly
or wrongly) idolatry, and miracles which seemed
to them (rightly or wrongly) impostures; that
the clergy interfered perpetually with the sanctity
of family life, as well as with the welfare of the
state : that their evil counsels, and specially those
of the Jesuits, had been patent and potent causes
of much of the misrule and misery of Louis
XIV.'s and XV.'s reigns: and that with all these
heavy counts against them, their morality was
not such as to make other men more moral; and
was not—at least among the hierarchy—improving,
or likely to improve. To a Mazarin, a De Retz,
a Richelieu (questionable men enough) had succeeded a Dubois, a Rohan, a Lomenie de Brienne,
a Maury, a Talleyrand; and at the revolution of
1789 thoughtful Frenchmen asked, once and for all,

what was to be done with a Church of which these
were the hierophants?

Whether these complaints affected the French
Church as a "religious" institution, must depend
entirely on the meaning which is attached to the
word religion : that they affected her on scientific,
rational, and moral grounds, independent of any
merely political one, is as patent as that the attack
based on them was one-sided, virulent, and often
somewhat hypocritical, considering the private
morals of many of the assailants. We know—or
ought to know—that within that religion which
seemed to the 'philosophes' (so distorted and defaced had it become) a nightmare dream, crushing
the life out of mankind, there lie elements divine,
eternal; necessary for man in this life and the life
to come. But we are bound to ask—Had they
a fair chance of knowing what we know? Have
we proof that their hatred was against all religion,
or only against that which they saw around them?
Have we proof that they would have equally hated,
had they been in permanent contact with them,
creeds more free from certain faults which seemed

to them, in the case of the French Church, ineradicable and inexpiable ? Till then, we must have charity—which is justice—even for the 'philosophes' of the eighteenth century.

This view of the case had been surely overlooked by M. De Tocqueville, when he tried to explain by the fear of revolutions, the fact that both in America and in England, "while the boldest political doctrines of the eighteenth century philosophers have been adopted, their anti-religious doctrines have made no way."

He confesses that, "Among the English, French irreligious philosophy had been preached, even before the greater part of the French philosophers were born. It was Bolingbroke who set up Voltaire. Throughout the eighteenth century infidelity had celebrated champions in England. Able writers and profound thinkers espoused that cause, but they were never able to render it triumphant as in France." Of these facts there can be no doubt : but the cause which he gives for the failure of infidelity will surely sound new and strange to those who know the English literature and history of that century. It was, he says, "inasmuch as all those who had anything to fear from revolutions, eagerly came to the rescue of the established faith." Surely there was no talk of revolutions; no wish, expressed or concealed, to overthrow either government or society, in the aristocratic clique to whom English infidelity was confined. Such was, at least, the opinion of Voltaire, who boasted that "All the works of the modern philosophers together would never make as much noise in the world as was made in former days by the disputes of the Cordeliers about the shape of their sleeves and hoods." If (as M. De Tocqueville says) Bolingbroke set up Voltaire, neither master nor pupil had any more leaning than Hobbes had toward a democracy which was not dreaded in those days, because it had never been heard of. And if (as M. De Tocqueville heartily allows) the English apologists of Christianity triumphed, at least for the time being, the cause of their triumph must be sought in the plain fact, that such men as Berkeley, Butler, and Paley, each according to his light, fought the battle fairly, on the common ground of reason and philosophy, instead of on that of tradition and authority ; and that the forms of Christianity current in England — whether Quaker, Puritan, or Anglican—offended, less than that current in France, the common-sense and the human instincts of the many, or of the sceptics themselves.]

But the eighteenth century saw another movement, all the more powerful, perhaps, because it was continually changing its shape, even its purpose ; and gaining fresh life and fresh adherents with every change. Propagated at first by men of the school of Locke, it became at last a protest against the materialism of that school, on behalf of all that is, or calls itself, supernatural and mysterious. Abjuring, and honestly, all politics, it found itself sucked into the political whirlpool in spite of itself, ·as all human interests which have any life in them must be at last. It became an active promoter of, the Revolution ; then it helped to destroy the Revolution, when that had, under Napoleon, become a levelling despotism ; then it helped, as actively, to keep revolutionary principles alive, after the reaction of 1815 :—a Protean institution, whose power we in England are as apt to undervalue, as the Governments of the Continent were apt, during the eighteenth century, to exaggerate it. I mean, of course, Freemasonry, and the secret societies which, honestly and honourably disowned by Freemasonry, yet have either copied it, or actually sprung out of it. In England, Freemasonry never was, it seems, more than a liberal and respectable benefit-club; for secret societies are needless for any further purposes, amid free institutions and a free press. But on the Continent during the eighteenth century, Freemasonry excited profound suspicion and fear on the part of statesmen who knew perfectly well their friends from their foes; and whose precautions were, from their point of view, justified by the results.

I shall not enter into the deep question of the origin of Freemasonry. One uninitiate, as I am, has no right to give an opinion on the great questions of the mediæval lodge of Kilwinning and its Scotch degrees; on the seven Templars, who, after poor Jacques Molay was burnt at Paris, took refuge on the Isle of Mull, in Scotland, found there another Templar and brother Mason, ominously named Harris, took to the trowel in earnest, and revived the Order;—on the Masons who built Magdeburg Cathedral in 876; on the English Masons assembled in Pagan times, by " St. Albone, that worthy knight ;" on the revival of English Masonry by Edwin, son of Athelstan; on Magnus Grecus, who had been at the building of Solomon's Temple, and taught Masonry to Charles Martel; on the pillars Jachin and Boaz; on the masonry of Hiram of Tyre, and indeed of Adam himself, of whose first fig-leaf the masonic apron may be a type—on all these matters I dare no more decide, than on the making of the Trojan Horse, the birth of Romulus and Remus, or the incarnation of Vishnoo.

All I dare say is, that Freemasonry emerges in its present form into history and fact, seemingly about the beginning of George the First's reign, among English gentlemen and noblemen, notably in four lodges in the city of London: (1) at the " Goose and Gridiron " alehouse in St. Paul's Churchyard ; (2) at the " Crown" alehouse near Drury-lane ; (3) at the " Apple Tree" tavern near

Covent Garden; (4) at the " Rummer and Grapes " tavern, in Charnel-row, Westminster. That its principles were brotherly love and good fellowship, which included in those days port, sherry, claret, and punch; that it was founded on the ground of mere humanity, in every sense of the word; being (as was to be expected from the temper of the times) both aristocratic and liberal, admitting to its ranks virtuous gentlemen, "obliged," says an old charge, " only to that religion wherein all men agree, leaving their particular opinions to themselves: that is, to be good men and true, or men of honour and honesty, by whatever denominations or persuasions they may be distinguished ; whereby Masonry becomes the centre of union, and means of conciliating true friendship among persons, that otherwise must have remained at a distance."

Little did the honest gentlemen who established or re-established their society on these grounds, and fenced it with quaint ceremonies, old or new, conceive the importance of their own act : we, looking at it from a distance, may see all that such a

I

society involved, which was quite new to the world just then ; and see, that it was the very child of the Ancien Regime—of a time when men were growing weary of the violent factions, political and spiritual, which had torn Europe in pieces for more than a century, and longed to say, " After all, we are all alike in one thing—for we are at least men."

Its spread through England and Scotland, and the seceding bodies which arose from it ; as well as the supposed Jacobite tendency of certain Scotch lodges, do not concern us here. The point interesting to us just now is, that Freemasonry was imported to the Continent exclusively by English and Scotch gentlemen and noblemen. Lord Derwentwater is said by some to have founded the " Loge Anglaise" in Paris in 1725—the Duke of Richmond one in his own castle of Aubigny shortly after. It was through Hanoverian influence that the movement seems to have spread into Germany : in 1733, for instance, the English Grand Master, Lord Strathmore, permitted eleven German gentlemen and good brethren to form a lodge in Hamburg. Into this English Society was Frederick the Great, when

Crown Prince, initiated, in spite of strict old Frederick William's objections, who had heard of it as an English invention, of irreligious tendency. Francis I. of Austria was made a Freemason at the Hague, Lord Chesterfield being in the chair, and then became a Master in London under the name of " Brother Lothringen," to the discontent of Maria Theresa, whose woman's wit saw farther than her husband. Englishmen and Scotchmen introduced the new Society into Russia and into Geneva. Sweden and Poland seem to have received it from France ; while, in the South, it seems to have been exclusively an English plant. Sackville, Duke of Middlesex, is said to have founded the first lodge at Florence in 1733, Lord Coleraine at Gibraltar and Madrid, one Gordon in Portugal ; and everywhere, at the commencement of the movement, we find either London or Scotland the mother-lodges, introducing on the Continent those liberal and humane ideas of which England was then considered, to her glory, as the only home left on earth.

But, alas! the seed sown grew up into strange

shapes, according to the soil in which it rooted.
False doctrine, heresy, and schism, according to
Herr Findel, the learned and rational historian
whom I have chiefly followed, defiled the new
Church from its infancy. " In France," so he be-
moans himself, " first of all there shot up that
baneful seed of lies and frauds, of vanity and pre-
sumption, of hatred and discord, the mischievous
high degrees; the misstatement that our order was
allied to the Templars, and existed at the time of
the Crusades; the removal of old charges, the
bringing in surreptitiously of a multitude of symbols and forms which awoke the love of secrecy;
knighthood; and, in fact, all which tended to poison
Freemasonry." Herr Findel seems to attribute these
evils principally to the " high degrees." It would
have been more simple to have attributed them to
the morals of the French noblesse in the days of
Louis Quinze. What could a corrupt tree bring
forth, but corrupt fruit ? If some of the early lodges,
like those of " La Félicité " and " L'Ancre," to which
women were admitted, resembled not a little the
Bacchic mysteries of old Rome, and like them called

for the interference of the police, still no great reform was to be expected, when those Sovereign Masonic Princes, the "Emperors of the East and West," quarrelled—knights of the East against knights of the West—till they were absorbed or crushed by the Lodge "Grand Orient," with Philippe Egalité, Duc de Chartres, as their grand master, and as his representative, the hero of the diamond necklace, and disciple of Count Cagliostro—Louis, Prince de Rohan.

But if Freemasonry, among the frivolous and sensual French noblesse, became utterly frivolous and sensual itself, it took a deeper, though a questionably fantastic form, among the more serious and earnest German nobility. Forgetful as they too often were of their duty to their peoples—tyrannical, extravagant, debauched by French opinions, French fashions, French luxuries, till they had begun to despise their native speech, their native literature, almost their native land, and to hide their native homeliness under a clumsy varnish of French outside civilization, which the years 1807–1813 rubbed off them again with a brush of iron—they were yet

Germans at heart; and that German instinct for the unseen—call it enthusiasm, mysticism, what you will, you cannot make it anything but a human fact, and a most powerful, and (as I hold) most blessed fact—that instinct for the unseen, I say, which gives peculiar value to German philosophy, poetry, art, religion, and above all to German family life, and which is just the complement needed to prevent our English common-sense, matter-of-fact Lockism from degenerating into materialism—that was only lying hidden, but not dead, in the German spirit.

With the Germans, therefore, Freemasonry assumed a nobler and more earnest shape. Dropping, very soon, that Lockite and Philosophe tone which had perhaps recommended it to Frederick the Great in his youth, it became mediævalist and mystic. It craved after a resuscitation of old chivalrous forms, if possible of the old chivalrous spirit, and the virtues of the knightly ideal, and the old German "biederkeit und tapferkeit," which were all defiled and overlaid by French fopperies. And not in vain; as no struggle after a noble aim, however confused or fantastic, is ever in vain. Free-

masonry was the direct parent of the Tugenbund,
and of those secret societies which freed Germany
from Napoleon. Whatever follies young members of
them may have committed ; whatever Jahn and his
Turnerei ; whatever the iron youths, with their iron
decorations and iron boot-heels; whatever, in a word,
may have been said or done amiss, in that childish-
ness which (as their own wisest writers often lament)
so often defaces the noble childlikeness of the German spirit, let it be always remembered that under
the impulse first given by Freemasonry, as much as
that given by such heroes as Stein and Scharnhorst,
Germany shook off the chains which had fallen on
her in her sleep ; and stood once more at Leipsic,
were it but for a moment, a free people alike in
body and in soul.

Remembering this, and the solid benefits which
Germany owed to Masonic influences, one shrinks
from saying much of the extravagances in which
its Masonry indulged before the French Revolution.
Yet they are so characteristic of the age, so significant to the student of human nature, that they
must be hinted at, though not detailed.

It is clear that Masonry was at first a movement confined to the aristocracy, or at least to the most educated classes; and clear, too, that it fell in with a temper of mind unsatisfied with the dry dogmatism into which the popular creeds had then been frozen—unsatisfied with their own Frenchified foppery and pseudo-philosophy—unsatisfied with want of all duty, purpose, noble thought, or noble work. With such a temper of mind it fell in : but that very temper was open (as it always is) to those dreams of a royal road to wisdom and to virtue, which have haunted, in all ages, the luxurious and the idle.

Those who will, may read enough, and too much, of the wonderful secrets in nature and science and theosophy, which men expected to find and did not find in the higher degrees of Masonry, till old Voss—the translator of Homer—had to confess, that after "trying for eleven years to attain a perfect knowledge of the inmost penetralia, where the secret is said to be, and of its invisible guardians," all he knew was that "the documents which he had to make known to the initiated were nothing more than a well got-up farce."

But the mania was general. The high-born and the virtuous expected to discover some panacea for their own consciences in what Voss calls, " A multitude of symbols, which are ever increasing the further you penetrate, and which are made to have a moral application through some arbitrary twisting of their meaning, as if I were to attempt expounding the chaos on my writing-desk."   .

A rich harvest field was an aristocracy in such a humour, for quacks of every kind ; richer even than that of France, in that the Germans were at once more honest and more earnest, and therefore to be robbed more easily.   The carcass was there: and the birds of prey were gathered together.

Of Rosa, with his lodge of the Three Hammers, and his Potsdam gold-making ;—of Johnson, alias Leuchte, who passed himself off as a Grand Prior sent from Scotland to resuscitate the order of Knights Templars; who informed his disciples that the Grand Master Von Hund commanded 26,000 men ; that round the convent (what convent, does not appear) a high wall was erected, which was guarded day and night ; that the English navy was in the hands of the Order ; that they had MSS. written by Hugo de Paganis (a mythic hero who often figures in these fables); that their treasure was in only three places in the world, in Ballenstadt, in the icy mountains of Savoy, and in China; that whosoever drew on himself the displeasure of the Order, perished both body and soul ; who degraded his rival Rosa to the sound of military music, and after having had, like every dog, his day, died in prison in the Wartburg ;—of the Rosicrucians, who were accused of wanting to support and advance the Catholic religion — one would think the accusation was very unnecessary, seeing that their actual dealings were with the philosopher's stone, and the exorcism of spirits ; and that the first apostle of the new golden Rosicrucian order, one Schröpfer, getting into debt, and fearing exposure, finished his life in an altogether un-catholic manner at Leipsic in 1774, by shooting himself;—of Keller and his Urim and Thummim ;— of Wöllner (who caught the Crown Prince Frederick William) with his three names of Chrysophiron, Heliconus, and Ophiron, and his fourth name of Ormesus Magnus, under which all the brethren were

to offer up for him solemn prayers and intercessions ;
—of Baron Heinrich Von Ekker and Eckenhofen,
gentleman of the bed-chamber and counsellor of
the Duke of Coburg Saalfeld, and his Jewish col-
league Hirschmann, with their Asiatic brethren and
order named Ben Bicca, Cabalistic and Talmudic ;—
of the Illuminati, and poor Adam Weisshaupt, Professor of Canon and National Law at Ingoldstadt in
Bavaria, who set up what he considered an Anti-
Jesuitical order on a Jesuit model, with some
vague hope, according to his own showing, of
" perfecting the reasoning powers interesting to
mankind, spreading the knowledge of sentiments
both humane and social, checking wicked inclina-
tions, standing up for oppressed and suffering virtue
against all wrong, promoting the advancement of
men of merit, and in every way facilitating the
acquirement of knowledge and science ;"—of this
honest silly man, and his attempts to carry out all
his fine projects by calling himself Spartacus, Bavaria Achaia, Austria Egypt, Vienna Rome, and
so forth ;—of Knigge, who picked his honest brains,
quarrelled with him, and then made money and

fame out of his plans, for as long as they lasted;—of Bode, the knight of the lilies of the valley, who, having caught Duke Ernest of Saxe Gotha, was himself caught by Knigge, and his eight, nine, or more ascending orders of unwisdom;—and finally of the Jesuits who, really with considerable excuses for their severity, fell upon these poor foolish Illuminati in 1784 throughout Bavaria, and had them exiled or imprisoned;—of all this you may read in the pages of Dr. Findel, and in many another book. For, forgotten as they are now, they made noise enough in their time.

And so it befell, that this eighteenth century, which is usually held to be the most "materialistic" of epochs, was, in fact, a most "spiritualistic" one; in which ghosts, demons, quacks, philosophers' stones, enchanters' wands, mysteries and mummeries, were as fashionable—as they will probably be again some day.

You have all heard of Cagliostro—"pupil of the sage Althotas, foster-child of the Scheriff of Mecca, probable son of the last king of Trebizond; named also Acharat, and 'Unfortunate child of

Nature;' by profession healer of diseases, abo-
lisher of wrinkles, friend of the poor and impotent;
grand-master of the Egyptian Mason-lodge of
High Science, spirit-summoner, gold-cook, Grand-
Cophta, prophet, priest, Thaumaturgic moralist, and
swindler"—born Giuseppe Balsamo of Palermo ;—
of him, and of his lovely Countess Seraphina—née
Lorenza Feliciani ? You have read what Goethe—
and still more important, what Mr. Carlyle has
written on him, as on one of the most significant
personages of the age ? Remember, then, that
Cagliostro was no isolated phenomenon; that
his success—nay, his having even conceived the
possibility of success in the brain that lay within
that " brass-faced, bull-necked, thick-lipped " head—
was made possible by public opinion. Had Cagliostro lived in our time, public opinion would have
pointed out to him other roads to honour—on which
he would doubtless have fared as well. For when
the silly dace try to be caught and hope to be
caught, he is a foolish pike who cannot gorge them.
But the method most easy for a pike-nature like
Cagliostro's, was in the eighteenth century, as it

may be in the latter half of the nineteenth, to trade, in a materialist age, on the unsatisfied spiritual cravings of mankind. For what do all these phantasms betoken, but a generation ashamed of its own materialism, sensuality, insincerity, ignorance, and striving to escape therefrom by any and every mad superstition which seemed likely to give an answer to the awful questions—What are we, and where? and to lay to rest those instincts of the unseen and infinite around it, which tormented it like ghosts by day and night: a sight ludicrous or pathetic, according as it is looked on by a cynical or a human spirit.

It is easy to call such a phenomenon absurd, improbable. It is rather rational, probable, say certain to happen. Rational, I say; for the reason of man tells him, and has always told him, that he is a supernatural being, if by nature is meant that which is cognizable by his five senses: that his coming into this world, his relation to it, his exit from it — which are the three most important facts about him—are supernatural, not to be explained by any deductions from the impressions

of his senses. And I make bold to say, that the re-
cent discoveries of physical science—notably those of
embryology—go only to justify that old and general
belief of man. If man be told that the microscope
and scalpel show no difference, in the first stage
of visible existence, between him and the lower
mammals, then he has a right to answer—as he will
answer—So much the worse for the microscope and
scalpel : so much the better for my old belief, that
there is beneath my birth, life, death, a substratum
of supernatural causes, imponderable, invisible,
unknowable by any physical science whatsoever.
If you cannot render me a reason how I came
hither, and what I am, I must go to those who
will render me one. And if that craving be not
satisfied by a rational theory of life, it will
demand satisfaction from some magical theory ;
as did the mind of the eighteenth century,
when, revolting from materialism, it fled to
magic, to explain the ever-astounding miracle
of life.

The old Regime. Will our age, in its turn, ever
be spoken of as an old Regime ? Will it ever be

spoken of as a Regime at all; as an organized, orderly system of society and polity; and not merely as a chaos, an anarchy, a transitory struggle, of which the money-lender has been the real guide and lord?

But at least it will be spoken of as an age of progress, of rapid developments, of astonishing discoveries.

Are you so sure of that? There was an age of progress once. But what is our age—what is all which has befallen since 1815—save after-swells of that great storm, which are weakening and lulling into heavy calm? Are we on the eve of stagnation? Of a long check to the human intellect? Of a new Byzantine era, in which little men will discuss, and ape, the deeds which great men did in their forefathers' days?

What progress—it is a question which some will receive with almost angry surprise—what progress has the human mind made since 1815?

If the thought be startling, do me the great honour of taking it home, and verifying for yourselves its truth or its falsehood. I do not say that it is altogether true. No proposition concerning human things, stated so broadly, can be. But see for yourselves, whether it is not at least more true than false; whether the ideas, the discoveries, of which we boast most in the nineteenth century, are not really due to the end of the eighteenth. Whether other men did not labour, and we have only entered into their labours. Whether our positivist spirit, our content with the collecting of facts, our dread of vast theories, is not a symptom—wholesome, prudent, modest, but still a symptom—of our consciousness that we are not as our grandfathers were; that we can no longer conceive great ideas, which illumine, for good or evil, the whole mind and heart of man, and drive him on to dare and suffer desperately.

Railroads? Electric telegraphs? All honour to them in their place: but they are not progress; they are only the fruits of past progress. No outward and material thing is progress; no machinery causes progress; it merely spreads and makes popular the results of progress. Progress is inward, of the soul. And, therefore, improved

K

constitutions, and improved book-instruction—now miscalled education—are not progress: they are at best only fruits and signs thereof. For they are outward, material; and progress, I say, is inward. The self-help and self-determination of the independent soul—that is the root of progress; and the more human beings who have that, the more progress there is in the world. Give me a man who, though he can neither read nor write, yet dares think for himself, and do the thing he believes: that man will help forward the human race more than any thousand men who have read, or written either, a thousand books apiece, but have not dared to think for themselves. And better for his race, and better, I believe, in the sight of God, the confusions and mistakes of that one sincere brave man, than the second-hand and cowardly correctness of all the thousand.

As for the "triumphs of science," let us honour, with astonishment and awe, the genius of those who invented them; but let us remember that the things themselves are as a gun or a sword, with which we can kill our enemy, but with which also our enemy can kill us. Like all out-ward and material things, they are equally fit for good and for evil. In England here—they have been as yet, as far as I can see, nothing but bless-ings: but I have my very serious doubts whether they are likely to be blessings to the whole human race, for many an age to come. I can conceive them—may God avert the omen !—the instruments of a more crushing executive centralization, of a more utter oppression of the bodies and souls of men, than the world has yet seen. I can conceive —may God avert the omen !—centuries hence, some future world-ruler sitting at the junction of all railroads, at the centre of all telegraph-wires —a world-spider in the omphalos of his world-wide web ; and smiting from thence everything that dared to lift its head, or utter a cry of pain, with a swiftness and surety to which the craft of a Justinian or a Philip II. was but clumsy and impotent.

All, all outward things, be sure of it, are good or evil, exactly as far as they are in the hands of good men or of bad.

Moreover, paradoxical as it may seem, railroads and telegraphs, instead of inaugurating an era of progress, may possibly only retard it. "Rester sur un grand succès," which was Rossini's advice to a young singer who had achieved a triumph, is a maxim which the world often follows, not only from prudence, but from necessity. They have done so much that it seems neither prudent nor possible to do more. They will rest and be thankful.

Thus, gunpowder and printing made rapid changes enough ; but those changes had no further development. The new art of war, the new art of literature, remained stationary, or rather receded and degenerated, till the end of the eighteenth century.

And so it may be with our means of locomotion and intercommunion, and what depends on them. The vast and unprecedented amount of capital, of social interests, of actual human intellect invested—I may say locked up—in these railroads, and telegraphs, and other triumphs of industry and science, will not enter into competition against themselves. They will not set themselves free to seek new discoveries in directions which are often actually opposed to their own, always foreign to it. If the money of thousands are locked up in these great works, the brains of hundreds of thousands, and of the very shrewdest too, are equally locked up therein likewise; and are to be subtracted from the gross material of social development, and added (without personal fault of their owners, who may be very good men) to the dead weight of vested selfishness, ignorance, and dislike of change.

Yes. A Byzantine and stationary age is possible yet. Perhaps we are now entering upon it; an age in which mankind shall be satisfied with the "triumphs of science," and shall look merely to the greatest comfort (call it not happiness) of the greatest number; and, like the debased Jews of old, "having found the life of their hand, be therewith content," no matter in what mud-hole of slavery and superstition.

But one hope there is, and more than a hope, one certainty, that however satisfied enlightened

public opinion may become with the results of
science, and the progress of the human race, there
will be always a more enlightened private opinion,
or opinions, which will not be satisfied therewith at
all; a few men of genius, a few children of light,
it may be a few persecuted, and a few martyrs for
new truths, who will wish the world not to rest and
be thankful, but to be discontented with itself,
ashamed of itself, striving and toiling upward,
without present hope of gain, till it has reached
that unknown goal which Bacon saw afar off,
and, like all other heroes, died in faith, not having
received the promises, but seeking still a polity
which has foundations, whose builder and maker
is God.

These will be the men of science, whether physical or spiritual. Not merely the men who
utilize and apply that which is known (useful
as they plainly are), but the men who themselves discover that which was unknown, and are
generally deemed useless, if not hurtful, to their
race. They will keep the sacred lamp burning
unobserved in quiet studies, while all the world is

gazing only at the gaslights flaring in the street. They will pass that lamp on from hand to hand, modestly, almost stealthily, till the day comes round again, when the obscure student shall be discovered once more to be, as he has always been, the strongest man on earth. For they follow a mistress whose footsteps may often slip, yet never fall; for she walks forward on the eternal facts of Nature, which are the acted will of God. A giantess she is: young indeed, but humble as yet; cautious and modest beyond her years. She is accused of trying to scale Olympus, by some who fancy that they have already scaled it themselves, and will, of course, brook no rival in their fancied monopoly of wisdom.

The accusation, I believe, is unjust. And yet science may scale Olympus after all. Without intending it, almost without knowing it, she may find herself hereafter upon a summit of which she never dreamed; surveying the universe of God in the light of Him who made it and her, and remakes them both for ever and ever. On that summit she may stand hereafter, if only she goes on, as she goes now, in humility and in patience ; doing the duty which lies nearest her ; lured along the upward road, not by ambition, vanity, or greed, but by reverent curiosity for every new pebble, and flower, and child, and savage, around her feet.

THE END.

LONDON : R. CLAY, SON, AND TAYLOR, PRINTERS.

www.ingramcontent.com/pod-product-compliance
Lightning Source LLC
Chambersburg PA
CBHW020558270326
41927CB00006B/891